meeting the **professional standards framework**

# Primary Languages

## Effective Learning and Teaching

# Achieving

## QTS

meeting the **professional standards framework**

# Primary Languages

## Effective Learning and Teaching

## Cynthia Martin

LearningMatters

Acknowledgements
The author would like to thank Christina Skarbek for generously sharing trainee activities for Chapter 6 and Lid King for kind permission to use his diagram in Appendix 5. She also acknowledges early suggestions from Glynis Rumley, Tara Deevoy and John Bald. Thanks are additionally due to Louise Pagden for practical activities for developing Intercultural Understanding and Ros Venables for thoughts on the qualities of a subject leader.

First published in 2008 by Learning Matters Ltd.

*British Library Cataloguing in Publication Data*
A CIP record for this book is available from the British Library.

ISBN: 978 1 84445 138 8

Cover design by Topics.
Text design by Code 5 Design Associates Ltd.
Project management by Deer Park Productions, Tavistock
Typeset by PDQ Typesetting Ltd, Newcastle under Lyme
Printed and bound in Great Britain by Bell & Bain Ltd, Glasgow

Learning Matters
33 Southernhay East
Exeter EX1 1NX
Tel: 01392 215560
info@learningmatters.co.uk
www.learningmatters.co.uk

# Contents

# The Author

Cynthia Martin is Senior Lecturer in Modern Languages Education at the Institute of Education, The University of Reading, where she is responsible for the Primary Languages programme. Cynthia has extensive experience of Primary Languages, having worked in the field as a researcher, curriculum developer, and teacher trainer for nearly twenty years. She has also taught French in a local primary school and works regularly with primary and secondary teachers in her role as Co-ordinator of two NACELL Regional Support Groups. She is a National Trainer for the Key Stage 2 Framework for Languages and a Comenius Primary Languages Consultant for CILT, The National Centre for Languages. Cynthia has had first hand involvement in all national initiatives related to Primary Languages and works closely with external agencies such as CILT, the TDA, QCA, Ofsted, and the British Council. A longstanding participant of the Early Language Learning Advisory Forum, she is also Chair of the Primary Special Interest Group for the Association for Language Learning and a member of ALL's Executive Council. Cynthia is President-elect for ALL for 2008–09.

# About this book

This book will introduce you to the rationale underpinning Primary Languages (PL) teaching in England. The main body is targeted at specialist trainees on either postgraduate or undergraduate courses of initial teacher training who are aspiring to be Primary Languages Co-ordinators. The majority of these will be participating in the multi-lateral Primary Languages Initial Teacher Training Project, funded by the Training and Development Agency for Schools (TDA), which incorporates a four-week teaching placement abroad. In addition, the book is relevant for generalist primary trainees, who are interested in becoming effective primary class teachers of languages, but who may not intend to take on the prime responsibility of the subject leadership role. The book is also intended to support teacher trainers, who may be relatively new to the field of Primary Languages, by providing suggestions for readings, and module activities as part of a training programme. The many references to relevant research will be especially helpful for trainees working at Masters (M) level in their assignments and will support tutors from a teaching rather than academic background. The practical aspects of this book will also be useful for Newly Qualified Teachers (NQTs) and other professionals already in service, including Higher Level Teaching Assistants (HLTAs) and native speakers.

Although historically languages have been the preserve of the secondary phase in England, the advent of the National Languages Strategy (DfES, 2002) and the subsequent Languages Review undertaken by Lord Dearing (DCSF, 2007), recommended that languages should become a statutory part of the primary curriculum in 2010. As a means of support, the Key Stage 2 Framework for Languages (DfES, 2005; DCSF, 2007) and the new QCA schemes of work for Key Stage 2 French, German and Spanish (QCA, 2007), together with the TDA/CILT Teacher Trainee Support Materials (TDA/CILT, 2008), are central to this book. It is assumed throughout that readers will regularly access the CILT Primary Languages Training Zone at www.primarylanguages.org.uk and many of the suggested reflective and practical tasks are based on materials to be found there. Some of the tasks can be undertaken in advance, others are designed to be part of a teaching session, and others to contribute to independent study following on from tuition.

Primary Languages are a specifically 'primary' undertaking, and as such there are references to Excellence and Enjoyment (DfES, 2003a) and Every Child Matters (DfES, 2004). Finally, as this is a book for primary teacher trainees, there are clear links to the Professional Standards for Qualified Teacher Status (2007).

Each chapter of this book includes the following features:

- chapter objectives at the start of each chapter;
- clear links to the Professional Standards for Qualified Teacher Status;
- links to the Key Stage 2 Framework for Languages (DfES, 2005; DCSF, 2007), the new Schemes of Work for Key Stage 2 Languages (QCA, 2007) and TDA/CILT Teacher Trainee Support Materials (TDA/CILT, 2008), where appropriate;
- practical and reflective tasks within each chapter;
- a summary of key points;

- moving on (taking trainees forward from where the chapter finishes and looking at the next step, e.g. professional development/induction year);
- further reading and useful websites, providing both a theoretical and practical perspective linked to the theme of each chapter.

Each chapter addresses different aspects related to teaching and learning Primary Languages with concrete examples. The chapters are sequenced in a manner suitable for delivery of a Primary Languages training module in a Higher Education Institution and offer a possible framework for teacher trainers. Where appropriate, chapters incorporate references to current research. Most examples use French, as this continues to dominate language learning in primary schools in England. Primary teachers are typically excellent ICT practitioners and it is assumed throughout that where the interactive whiteboard, for example, could be used, any suggestion will be suitably adapted.

A glossary of important terms and common acronyms relating to the field of Primary Languages is provided, together with a reference list of useful titles for both trainees and their tutors.

# 1
# Setting the scene

**By the end of this chapter you will have:**

- become aware of the international context for current Primary Languages initiatives;
- considered significant milestones in the recent history of Primary Languages in England;
- understood what the term Primary Languages stands for;
- become aware of key documents and developments in the field.

You need to have an awareness of the international and national context so that you can fully appreciate what you will see being taught in school. This background will enable you to consider how far practice in the schools in which you are training relates to policy and research.

This chapter addresses the following Professional Standards for QTS:

**Q3a, Q14, Q15**

## Why Primary Languages? The European context

In 1995 the European Commission's White Paper on Education and Training (EC, 1995), emphasised the importance of children learning at least two foreign languages before upper secondary education. In 2002 the United Kingdom joined the European Centre for Modern Languages (ECML), which supports the implementation of language education policies based on the recommendations of the Council of Europe. In March 2002 a meeting in Barcelona of EU heads of state reiterated the call for at least two foreign languages to be taught from an early age. This was followed in 2003 by the adoption of an Action Plan to *promote language learning and linguistic diversity* (EC, 2003). No fewer than 45 actions in three broad areas were proposed for the period 2004–06.

1. To **extend the benefits** of language learning to **all** citizens as a **lifelong** activity.
2. To improve the **quality** of language teaching at all levels.
3. To build within Europe an environment favourable to languages.

These developments form the European backdrop against which the National Languages Strategy *Languages for all: Languages for life* (DfES, 2002) can be set.

## Multilingualism, monolingualism, plurilingualism

Multilingualism refers both to a person's ability to use several languages and to the coexistence of different language communities within one geographical area, as is the case in many of the cities in the UK. It is the European Commission's policy to promote a climate that is conducive to the full expression of all languages, in which the teaching and learning of a variety of languages can flourish. The Commission's long-term objective is to increase individual multilingualisms, until all citizens have practical skills in at least two languages in addition to their mother tongue (EC, 2005).

Johnstone (1994) made the point that in many parts of the world, bilingualism or multilingualism is the norm and knowing only one language, monolingualism, is the exception. But for many years in the UK, the situation was typically perceived as the reverse, with monolingualism accepted as the norm, and bilingualism and multilingualism viewed as the 'problem'.

**Plurilingualism** is a concept developed by the Council of Europe to refer to the totality of an individual's linguistic competences in and across different languages, which develops throughout life. In 2005 CILT surveyed community languages across England, Scotland and Wales, producing a booklet in 2006 entitled *Positively Plurilingual*, which highlights the major linguistic asset which the UK possesses in its multicultural population, which if developed wisely and inclusively alongside English and other languages, has the potential to benefit society as a whole as well as enhancing the life chances of individual children. Its introduction states.

> *As a nation seeking to play a key role in global trade and diplomacy, we need to be able to draw on a diverse range of languages to further our strategic and economic aims: and these are already represented among the languages spoken by our school children. Yet, in our haste to ensure they acquire good English, we frequently miss the opportunity to ensure they maintain and develop their skills in their other languages too. Rather than thinking in terms of an 'English-only' culture, we should be promoting 'English plus'.*
>
> (CILT, 2006, p1)

It is within this context of increasing awareness of the value of languages that the current initiatives in England are taking place. Providing good quality, early language learning is now a common aim across Europe, with some countries closer to achieving this than others. In most countries within mainland Europe, languages, in particular English, have become well established within the primary sector. In central and eastern Europe, as well as in Spain, Italy, Denmark and Iceland, there is a marked increase in the percentage of children in primary education who are learning at least one foreign language. English is the language most frequently taught, with German learned as the first foreign language in primary schools in the Baltic States, the Czech Republic, Hungary, Poland and Slovakia (Eurydice, 2005). This commitment has not traditionally been the case for languages in state maintained schools within England, where, apart from the pilot scheme *French from Eight* (see page 4), modern languages have been the preserve of either the secondary sector or independent schools.

Having noted this broader perspective, the nature of early language learning in England and its expansion now need to be considered in order to fully understand Primary Languages.

# What does Primary Languages mean?

For the purposes of this book, we need to distinguish between a learner's first language (L1), a second language (L2) and a foreign language (FL).

- A **first language (L1)** is the first language a child acquires, or the dominant language the child uses. It is sometimes called the learner's native language or mother tongue. Bilingual children may be said to have two first languages, or a first language and a strong second language.

- A **second language (L2)** is not the mother tongue of the learners but is a language spoken by a significant group in a community. So, an English speaker in parts of French-speaking Canada will learn French as an L2, on account of the significant population of French speakers in areas such as Quebec.
- A **foreign language (FL)** is the term used to refer to the learning of a language, typically through classroom instruction, which is spoken outside the boundaries of the country in which the learners live, and thus generally not widely used within the particular community. For most people in England, French, Spanish and German are foreign languages. Foreign languages tend to be limited to in-curriculum time and are rarely used outside the classroom.
- **Primary Languages (PL)** is the term given to the teaching of a language other than a child's first language (L1) or mother tongue, within curriculum time, in primary schools in England. It is important to note that the expression Primary Modern Foreign Languages (PMFL) is now less frequently used to describe language teaching in this phase. This has come about for a variety of reasons:
  - the need to ensure that Primary Languages are seen as something special, and quite distinct from language learning within the National Curriculum at secondary school, traditionally known as **Modern Foreign Languages (MFL)**\*;
  - the need to be inclusive and ensure that all languages, including community languages and non-European languages, have their rightful place;
  - the desire to make language learning something normal and accessible, not strange and 'foreign'.

\*It is noteworthy that the term 'languages', employed for some time for the primary phase, is now currently the recommended term for the secondary sector. Thus you will increasingly see references to the 'new secondary **languages curriculum**' (www.all-languages.org.uk), although Qualifications and Curriculum Authority documentation related to the Programme of Study and Attainment Targets for Key Stage 3 is expressed for the time being, at least, as Modern foreign languages (curriculum.qca.org.uk).

Primary Languages is separate from **English as an Additional Language (EAL)**, because EAL learners in multicultural Britain are operating within the target language culture, and for them, English, the host language, which is also the medium of school instruction, is an L2 (second language) rather than a foreign language.

# Exposure and motivation to learn languages

We need to bear in mind the contextual differences between young learners of English in other parts of Europe, and indeed, the world, and primary learners of foreign languages such as French, German and Spanish in UK school settings. Johnstone reminds us that:

> ...one of the major problems that foreign language teachers in the UK have always had to face has been that they have not only had to teach the language but in addition have had to accept responsibility for exposing their pupils to it.
>
> (Johnstone, 1994, p3)

In contrast, teachers of English as a foreign language in mainland Europe, in countries such as Holland for instance, know that children will also be regularly exposed to English out of school, through the internet, TV, pop songs, DVDs and CDs.

Furthermore, in countries such as Sweden or Norway, whose language is less widely known, the motivation to learn English is particularly high, as there are strong cultural, political and business reasons for learning it. As we saw earlier, native speakers of

English, especially, often have difficulty perceiving a need to learn any other language, as 'everyone speaks English'.

We should also note, when comparing developments on the continent of Europe, that children enter primary school at age six (for instance, in France, Germany, Spain and Italy), at age seven in Norway, Sweden and Finland, and at age four in the Netherlands. In England, Wales and Northern Ireland, the school-starting age is five.

# A short history of Primary Languages

There were a number of post-war initiatives to introduce language learning, the most influential in England being the Nuffield Foundation/Schools Council pilot scheme *French from Eight.* The proposal to introduce languages in the early 1960s was a radical one, since it involved the extension of languages teaching in pilot schools **down** the age range, to 8–11 year olds, at a time when languages were considered an elite subject, offered only to the top sets in secondary grammar schools. In addition, it **widened the scope** to embrace children of **all abilities**, again at a period when there was no experience of teaching languages in mixed ability classes. Some 17,000 children participated in the scheme, which took place in selected primary schools and local authorities (LAs). This was also the first major intervention by government in the school curriculum.

This initiative was the subject of a long-term evaluation between 1964 and 1974 by the National Foundation for Educational Research (NFER). Children typically learned French for three years between the ages of 8 and 11. At the age of 13, their performance was compared with that of a control group of the same age who had started languages in secondary school at the usual age of 11. The children in the experimental group performed better in listening and speaking but those in the control group did better in reading and writing. By age 16, the latter group was still superior in reading and writing, and the experimental group had lost their advantage in the oracy skills. These findings, combined with others, led the NFER team to conclude that no substantial gains in later attainment in secondary school could be demonstrated.

Burstall and colleagues stated unambiguously that:

> It is difficult to resist the conclusion that the weight of evidence has combined with the balance of opinion to tip the scales against a possible expansion of the teaching of French in primary schools.
>
> (Burstall et al., 1974, p246)

Consequently, the pilot scheme was not extended, although the validity of the findings were disputed (Gamble and Smalley, 1975; Buckby, 1976; Hoy, 1977). With the exception of areas where LAs were particularly committed to Primary Languages, as in Sussex and Surrey, or in a few schools where individual enthusiasts carried on, primary French died out.

However, the modern story of Primary Languages starts in the late 1980s and early 1990s, at a time when a number of fresh projects were being launched both in the UK and elsewhere in Europe, and indeed, internationally. In Scotland, where transfer to S1, the first year of secondary schooling, occurs at 12, a year later than in England, the Modern Languages in the Primary School (MLPS) pilot was beginning, eventually to be generalised across the whole of Scotland. In 1989 each pilot consisted of a secondary school and its associated primaries, so that the issues of continuity and progression could be addressed within the timescale, a major feature of the project. Six secondary schools and their associated primaries began in Phase 1, and in 1990, Phase 2 included a further six secondaries together with their primaries. Thus, 12 secondary schools and 76 primaries were involved, offering four languages between them. Evaluated by Low et al. (1993) and with a Final Report by Low et al. (1995), this national project, and others, notably in the Strathclyde region, have provided numerous lessons for practitioners and policy makers south of the border.

Nonetheless, modern languages continued to be excluded as a statutory primary school subject in England, mainly owing to the view that there were insufficient teachers with appropriate expertise (Dearing, 1993). Indeed, in 1990 the Modern Foreign Languages Working Group had pointed out that:

> *full-scale teaching of foreign languages in primary schools...is not at present possible, not because children of this age cannot successfully learn languages but because very few teachers in primary schools are equipped to teach them.*
>
> (DES, 1990, p9)

Notwithstanding these doubts, there were several examples of initiatives of various sizes, notably in Richmond, the Early Teaching of a Modern Language (ETML) project, in Tameside in Manchester, the Primary into Secondary Modern Language (PRISM) scheme, in the Isle of Man and in East Sussex, which published *Salut la France* in 1989, a scheme of work for Year 6 children, to name but a few. One of the largest and most significant has been in Kent, where a project initially known as the Kent Primary French Project was launched in 1989 with the support of a full time project officer from Kent County Council/Kent Local Authority. This eventually expanded into languages other than French and over the course of two decades, substantial resources have been produced and several thousand primary teachers have received in-service training (INSET) and customised resources, to help them deliver Primary Languages in their schools.

Around 1990 a national pre-11 languages network, known as the Primary Languages Network (PLN), was set up and met twice a year, usually at CILT, to act as an independent forum for teacher trainers, academics, LA advisers, inspectors, policy makers and teachers involved in teaching languages to primary age children. In December 2003, in the light of the Government's intentions for the rapid expansion of Primary Languages, it was decided to bring the PLN under the official wing of CILT and the ELL Initiative (see page 6). The network's name was changed to the CILT Early Language Learning Advisory Forum (ELLAF) and it continues to meet twice annually, with national representatives from key agencies, in order to offer its views to decision makers on future policy developments in Primary Languages.

In 1992 the Association for Language Learning (ALL) and the National Association of Head Teachers (NAHT), which represents primary head teachers, held a joint conference in Coventry entitled *Primary Foreign Languages: a fresh impetus* (Trafford, 1992). Two policy statements were published as a result of the conference. The NAHT resolution called on the Government to make *progress towards the introduction of foreign language learning before the age of eleven* (Trafford 1992, p54). The ALL statement declared: *This Association strongly supports an early start to the study of modern foreign languages.* (Trafford 1992, p52).

Another significant date is 1994, when the Dearing committee recommended that approximately 20 per cent of curriculum time should be freed up to

> *teach optional content outside the statutory core of each subject and for non-National Curriculum work where appropriate, for example the introduction of a foreign language at Key Stage 2, where the school has relevant expertise.*
>
> (Dearing, 1994, p82)

In 1995 CILT carried out a survey of Primary Languages provision in England, Wales and Northern Ireland, which indicated that around 40 LAs had some kind of languages teaching in primary schools (CILT, 1995).

This was followed by a national inquiry into the UK's capability in languages, the Nuffield Inquiry (1998), once again funded by the Nuffield Foundation, to investigate the policies required to enable Britain to *fulfil its economic, strategic, social and the cultural aims and responsibilities and the aspirations of its citizens.* (Moys, 1998, p4). In the same year the Secretary of State announced that the primary curriculum would be slimmed down, with a consequent opportunity to *offer tasters in other subjects, including modern languages if [schools] wish* (DfEE, 1998).

Another key date is 1999, when the (then) Department for Education and Employment launched the Early Language Learning (ELL) initiative. Managed on behalf of the DfEE by CILT, now the National Centre for Languages but known at the time as the Centre for Information on Language Teaching and Research, in partnership with a number of agencies, this ELL Initiative included the founding of the National Advisory Centre on Early Language Learning (NACELL), to be based at CILT. The purpose of the ELL initiative was *to promote and develop the provision and quality of Modern Foreign Language learning in the primary sector*. This was to be achieved initially through the Good Practice Project, for which bids were invited from schools for a modest amount of funding to identify, develop and disseminate good practice in Primary Languages. Of 64 tenders, 18 'projects' were accepted and evaluated by Sharpe (2003). Interim findings were made available to the Qualifications and Curriculum Authority (QCA) in order to support the production of the non-statutory guidelines for Primary Languages in the revised Year 2000 National Curriculum. In fact, the ELL initiative, which ran from 1999 to March 2001, was extended with additional funding as the Developing Early Language Learning (DELL) projects from 2001 to 2003.

The millennium year was significant for a number of materials designed to provide non-statutory support for teachers. These were the Schemes of Work for Key Stage 2 in French, German and Spanish and Teacher's Guide, produced by the Qualifications and Curriculum Authority (QCA, 2000), which were created alongside the QCA feasibility study (2001). This latter study investigated the feasibility of implementing languages provision within Key Stage 2 and incorporated a review of national and international research into early school-based language learning (Martin, 2000a) and a survey of Primary Languages provision undertaken by the University of Warwick (Powell et al., 2001). This latter survey suggested that 21 per cent of maintained schools with Key Stage 2 children were offering some form of languages teaching at the time.

Possibly the document with the most widespread impact is the National Languages Strategy (DfES, 2002), which sets out the entitlement that all children in Key Stage 2 should have the opportunity to learn a language within curriculum time.

*Every child should have the opportunity throughout Key Stage 2 to study a foreign language and develop their interest in the culture of other nations. They should have access to high quality teaching and learning opportunities, making use of native speakers and e-learning. By age 11 they should have the opportunity to reach a recognised level of competence on the Common European Framework and for that achievement to be recognised through a national scheme.*

(DfES, 2002, p15)

This key publication had been anticipated the year before, in 2001, by the launch of a new development in initial teacher training, the Primary Languages Initial Teacher Training (ITT) Project. Many of you will be participating in this exciting initiative. Managed by the Teacher Training Agency (TTA), subsequently the Training and Development Agency for Schools (TDA), this project started with just five Higher Education Institutions (HEIs) in England, each of which was partnered with an *Institut Universitaire de Formation des Maîtres* (IUFM) in France. With each succeeding year, this initiative has continued to expand, both in size – there are now more than 40 HEIs involved – and in number of languages – as well as French, trainees can be preparing to teach Spanish, German, and Italian. Each of the HEIs is part-nered with a training institution in the target language country, and a unique feature of the training is the month's teaching placement abroad, to which we refer in Chapter 6.

As you will be aware from your primary training course, the primary curriculum was also undergoing change with the publication of new documents. In 2003 the DfES published *Speaking, Listening and Learning: Working with children at Key Stage 1 and Key Stage 2* (DfES, 2003b) and *Excellence and enjoyment: A strategy for primary schools* (DfES, 2003a), which placed a renewed emphasis on a combination of excellent teaching with the enjoy-ment of learning. This latter document included, among a number of case studies, the development of the National Languages Strategy and the Key Stage 2 entitlement. This was followed by *Every Child Matters: Change for children* (DfES, 2004).

# Recent developments

These developments formed the backdrop for the Key Stage 2 Framework for Languages (DfES, 2005; DCSF, 2007), which is the non-statutory guidance for languages in the primary phase. This Framework has had a phased introduction, with Parts 1 and 2 appearing in 2005 and Part 3 in 2007. The Framework is accompanied by an online portal, Primary Languages, a Training Zone, www.primarylanguages.org.uk, launched by CILT at the Primary Languages Show 2007, which is supporting the delivery of good practice in Primary Languages in a very exciting and dynamic way through DVD exemplars and further resources.

Alongside these initiatives has been the ongoing revision of the QCA schemes of work for Key Stage 2 Languages (QCA, 2007), to ensure that these are firmly rooted in excellent primary practice as well as linking to the Key Stage 2 Framework for Languages. Training modules and materials for primary teachers in post and for HLTAs have also been created. In 2006 the DfES, working with CILT, additionally commissioned a national training programme, entitled Training the Trainers, by means of which a group of National Trainers has been disseminating training on the Key Stage 2 Framework for Regional Trainers, who themselves are charged with cascading the training locally.

Throughout this process, the Department for Children, Schools and Families (DCSF) has been rigorous in commissioning further research to update earlier findings. Thus, in 2002, Canterbury Christchurch University was commissioned, with King's College London and

Manchester Metropolitan University, to carry out a survey of the provision of languages at Key Stage 2 (Driscoll et al., 2004). This survey indicated that some 44 per cent of schools with Key Stage 2 children were including some form of languages teaching, although only 3 per cent were teaching all four Key Stage 2 year groups. This research was followed up by a two-year evaluation of the Key Stage 2 Language Learning Pathfinders conducted by a team from Warwick and Reading Universities (Muijs et al., 2005).

By 2007, the Languages Review undertaken by Lord Dearing (2007), estimated that the number of primary schools offering languages had risen to around 70 per cent. The latest research involves a further quantitative survey of expanding provision of Primary Languages in Key Stage 2 by the NFER complemented by a three-year longitudinal study of Primary Languages learning at Key Stage 2 by the Open University, University of Southampton and Canterbury Christchurch University. These latter two studies commenced in 2006. Interim reports were published in 2007 and 2008. Final reports will be available in 2009.

**PRACTICAL TASK** PRACTICAL TASK PRACTICAL TASK PRACTICAL TASK PRACTICAL TASK

Consider any examples of Primary Languages teaching and learning which you have observed. This might be in your current teaching placement school, or you may have been involved in delivering or observing some Primary Languages before the start of your ITT course. With a partner or in a small group, discuss your observations and experiences and decide together whether or not you agree with the following statement.

*Primary Languages are distinctive. They are not simply a watered down version of the early secondary MFL curriculum.*

This book will assist you in investigating this growing body of support for Primary Languages as you undertake your initial teacher training. You need to be aware that the field of Primary Languages is a complex one, with a number of significant challenges. For example, Lord Dearing's Review of the 14–19 curriculum referred to the National Languages Strategy's proposal that languages should be taught in Key Stage 2 and highlighted the huge implications for staffing, training and associated costs.

> *The Government has put in hand measures to train and support existing primary teachers and teaching assistants and to equip 6000 new primary teachers with a language specialism. We propose that the provision for teacher support should be continued and where necessary extended at least until 2010.*
>
> (Dearing and King, 2006, p37)

The Primary Languages landscape is one of rapid change at the level of research, policy and practice and is also marked by an ever increasing number of resources and support mechanisms, which the following chapters will help you evaluate and implement successfully.

In the next chapter we consider the reasons for learning a language in the primary phase and discuss some of the aims and benefits. We suggest that in preparation for that chapter, you prepare the following task.

**REFLECTIVE TASK**

Brainstorm some of the reasons which are important to you about introducing a language before the age of 11. What benefits can you foresee either to individuals or more globally? Note these down ready for a discussion before you work on Chapter 2.

## A SUMMARY OF **KEY POINTS**

> **International developments: An increase in international and national expectations about the need for several languages at an early stage.**

> **We need to be careful in our definitions of language learning contexts and be aware of the special position of language learners in England on account of motivational and exposure issues.**

> **National developments: National Languages Strategy launched in 2002 stating that by 2010, children in Key Stage 2 will have an entitlement to learn a foreign language. Subsequently the Languages Review (Dearing, 2007) proposes that languages should become a statutory element in the primary curriculum at its next review.**

> **Policy to practice: Research indicates that the number of schools delivering Primary Languages is growing. There continues to be substantial investment in a sound infrastructure as recommended by Martin (2000a). The Key Stage 2 Framework for Languages and the new QCA schemes of work for languages are likely to have an increasing impact on what happens in classrooms and in what you will experience in schools.**

**MOVING** *ON* > > > > > > MOVING *ON* > > > > > > MOVING *ON*

You will need to keep abreast of developments as the National Languages Strategy is implemented, both during your initial training year, your induction period and throughout your career. To do so, we suggest that you start by reading some of the articles below. These will support you in writing your assignments, especially if these are at Masters level, and in your ongoing professional development.

**FURTHER READING** FURTHER READING **FURTHER READING** FURTHER READING

Dearing, R. and King, L. (2007) *Languages Review*. Nottingham: DfES publications. Ref: 00212-2007DOM-EN.

DfES (2002) *Languages for All: Languages for life. A strategy for England*. Nottingham: DfES Publications. Ref: DfES/0749/2002.

Moys, A. (ed) (1998) *Where are we going with languages?* London: Nuffield Foundation.

You can find four-page summaries of recent research as follows:

DCSF (2007) *Language learning provision at Key Stage 2: Findings from the 2006 survey*. Brief No: RBX02-07.

DCSF (2008) *Language learning provision at Key Stage 2: Findings from the 2007 survey*. Brief No: RBX 09-08.

DfES (2004) *The provision of foreign language learning for pupils at Key Stage 2*. Brief No: RB572.

DfES (2005) *Evaluation of the Key Stage 2 Language Learning Pathfinders*. Brief No: RB692.

## Useful websites

www.dcsf.gov.uk/research/data/uploadfiles/DCSF-RBX-09-08.pdf to access the NfER survey report, also on the NfER website www.nfer.org.uk/research

www.euractiv.com/en/culture/language-use-eu/article-137663 – European Policy summary

www.teachernet.gov.uk/publications to download the *Languages Review* or to order copies quoting reference 00212-2007DOM-EN

www.teachernet.gov.uk/publications to order National Languages Strategy, reference DfES 0749 2002

# 2

# Is younger better? Towards a rationale for teaching and learning languages in primary schools in England

**By the end of this chapter you will have:**

- considered the statement 'younger is better';
- become aware of some research evidence about the advantages and disadvantages of an early start;
- been introduced to a rationale for teaching and learning languages in primary schools;
- considered the benefits and purposes of learning languages in the primary school;
- reflected on different models of provision;

This chapter addresses the following Professional Standards for QTS:

**Q2, Q14, Q15**

## REFLECTIVE TASK

**Everyone knows the earlier you start, the easier it is.**

Tony Blair's statement in a lecture at Oxford University reflects a widespread view that languages are somehow easier to learn, if learned young and that therefore it is a 'good thing' to teach languages in primary school. Is this entirely true? Discuss Blair's statement.

- To what extent do you agree with him?
- What, if any, are the aspects of language learning which are easier?
- Are younger learners better at all tasks?
- Does the environment in which you learn a new language matter?
- Be ready to share your views.

In fact, in making claims about the benefits of starting languages young, we need to be quite clear about the different contexts in which early language learning may be taking place. As we saw in Chapter 1, one language learning context is that of children learning their mother tongue, or **L1**, surrounded by fluent speakers of the language who are constantly interacting with them at home, at play, in school, in the wider community. A second context is the naturalistic language learning situation in which a young learner may be growing up in an **L2** environment, and although their L1 may be used at home between parents and siblings within the family, the learner is surrounded by the L2 in most other situations, including as a medium of instruction at school, and is able to acquire the new language 'naturally'. Naturalistic contexts like these might be bilingual situations, when children accompany parents abroad and live in the target language country for a number of years, growing up hearing and seeing the L2 all around them and possibly being schooled via the medium of the L2. Thirdly, there are the language learning contexts similar to that which we find in the UK, in which the language being learned is a foreign language. In other words, it is not the language which is used by the majority of people in and outside the home and school. Learning the new language is limited to formal learning situations, in 'class time', and once the language lessons are over, other lessons in the curriculum continue in the mother tongue, in this case, English. In addition, there is no, or at most, little exposure to the new language outside of lessons, because the mother tongue dominates for all other purposes and can be found in the media and all around the learner all the time.

There are substantial numbers of research studies into the effect of starting age and several of these help us when we are considering Primary Languages learning in England. However, we must be cautious of making overambitious claims about the benefits and outcomes of an early start to language learning within the English school context of sparse exposure limited to lesson time. Many of the claims made by enthusiasts for an early start to school-based FL learning are, in fact, based on acquirers/learners in a different culture and context from that which pertain in the UK. We must be wary of making inappropriate or exaggerated claims for the environment of the primary school classroom, where the majority of learners share the same mother tongue and where there may be, say, 30 learners to one FL teacher. Clearly these cannot provide the same conditions as those experienced by young children who have moved to another country and are learning an L2 in a natural setting.

Instead we need to consider particularly the findings from research studies into instructed language learning in school-based settings where, for example, the lingua franca may, in fact, be English, and the motivation to learn a new language be weak. Studies based on English-speaking countries such as the USA, Australia and New Zealand may yield findings more appropriate to the situation in England. We have all heard statements such as 'Everyone speaks English!' It is understandable, perhaps, that in these kinds of contexts, the motivation to learn another language may be limited.

# Age and L2/FL learning

As we noted above, it is complex comparing studies which have considered different aspects of L2 and FL learning using different subject populations, in different language learning contexts, and employing different methods to measure learning. Findings on the effects of an early start still do not present a uniform picture. Hunt et al. sum up the Critical Period Hypothesis (CPH) thus:

> *The CPH which has given birth to the 'younger is better' claim, maintains that young children have a special instinctive capacity including both speech and morpho-syntactic development, that their brain has plasticity before it lateralizes and that they can acquire L2 in similar ways to their mother tongue (L1). As a result, it is a common assertion by those promoting early foreign language learning that age is an important factor contributing to success at school due to this special capacity.*
>
> (Hunt et al., 2005, p372)

An expert on the 'age question', Singleton (1989) suggests that the assumption that young learners possess natural attributes, which enable to them to acquire languages more efficiently than older learners, is part of 'folk wisdom' based on the speed at which young children master their L1, and the way they seem, when they emigrate, to acquire better pronunciation, and a more 'native' grammatical usage and word choice in another language than older family members.

Here are some other questions for you to discuss.

**REFLECTIVE TASK**

**Better at what?**

- Who does better if you match learners of **different ages** according to the **time** they have been learning the new language:
  - **older 'adult' beginner learners;**
  - **pre-11 younger learners? (our primary school population);**
  - **adolescents?**
- What do the better language learners do better at? Why might this be?

There is some research evidence to suggest that in an L2, naturalistic situation, young learners are likely to find it easier to learn the new language of the host country than adult beginners. In contrast, in formal learning situations, older beginners are often more efficient language learners. Oller and Nagato (1974) studied children in Japanese schools learning English in Grades 7, 9 and 11. At each level there were children who had already had six years of English prior to Grade 7, as well as some who did not start English until the later grades. At Grade 7 Oller and Nagato found that there was a significant difference in favour of those who had learned English before, but this difference decreased by Grade 9 and by Grade 11 was insignificant. This seemed to imply that older beginners are able to learn as much in five years as younger beginners do in eleven. Why might this be the case in formal educational settings?

Older learners may out-perform younger learners in the rate of language acquisition because they have a better grasp of grammatical patterns, which transfer from the L1 to the new language, as well as a much larger vocabulary in their first language than younger children (Ausubel, 1964; Hawkins, 1987; Collier, 1989). They may be particularly good at learning the syntax and morphology of the new language and at reading and writing. There are several reasons for this. For one thing, adult beginners are already experienced language learners, having skillfully acquired one language, their mother tongue, and can bring a variety of skills to bear on the process of learning a new language. Older beginners may be more capable of making conscious grammatical generalisations, whereas young learners have to discover syntactical rules through repeated exposure to models. They have developed greater cognitive maturity and have better general learning strategies, making use of metacognitive as well as cognitive strategies, and are more able to plan, monitor and evaluate their learning (Johnstone, 1994). Hence they may initially, at least, be more efficient. In addition, they often have good reasons for language learning, they know why they are doing it and may typically have a particular intention in mind, such as learning a language for business, travel or leisure purposes. Indeed, older learners often choose to learn a particular language rather than being required to do so, as children in school may be.

In other words, older learners may have:

- more efficient **learning strategies;**

- a more **mature conceptual map** of the world;
- a clearer sense of **reasons** for learning a FL.

So do young learners in school-based settings have **any** advantages?

**REFLECTIVE TASK**

- Whenever you have watched primary aged children learning a new language, have you noticed anything about their responses to songs, games, action rhymes, stories, new sounds to be repeated?
- In what ways does their response differ from older, secondary school language learners?

We do know that primary aged children are typically excellent mimics. They usually thoroughly enjoy rhymes and songs and having a go at speaking the new language. In contrast to post-11 language learners, they respond enthusiastically when experimenting with the sounds of the new language, which they are keen to imitate and echo back to the teacher, doing so accurately and without requiring much in the way of encouragement. Indeed, increasing age shows a decline in the quality of native-like pronunciation (Tahta et al., 1981). Younger language learners are typically superior at:

- mastering the development of the **phonological or sound system**;
- the ability to **identify/imitate sounds** closely and without inhibition.

Why do you think this is?

Children are usually prepared to take risks when trying out the new language, especially if we provide the appropriate environment. They are uninhibited, unembarrassed and less self-conscious than secondary age learners. They enjoy imitating a model, both pronunciation and intonation.

**REFLECTIVE TASK**

Bearing in mind the National Languages Strategy recommendation that children should have access to *high quality teaching and learning opportunities*, (DfES, 2002, p15), together with children's intuitive sensitivity to sound and ability to mimic, can you think of any implications for us as **teachers**, as regards pronunciation models?

# The time factor

We have seen that starting age determines levels of accuracy, particularly in pronunciation and the mastery of the phonetic system. Furthermore, the amount of time spent actively learning a foreign language is thought to be a significant factor in achieving high levels of proficiency (Radnai, 1996), so starting earlier provides learners with more time for language learning. A secondary beginner is unlikely to have as much time overall as a primary beginner. **Time for learning is crucial.**

A cautionary note:

- starting earlier **in school** does not **on its own** guarantee an advantage;
- **quality of teaching is crucial: the pronunciation model provided must be excellent**;
- *not* younger = better in **all circumstances over any timescale**.

# What are the benefits of early language learning?

Now let us turn our attention to what might be gained by well-taught Primary Languages lessons. Particularly those of you who will become Primary Languages Co-ordinators, will need to consider the benefits of Primary Languages as part of writing a languages policy for your school (see Chapter 8).

## REFLECTIVE TASK

(You will need large sheets of paper and marker pens.)

Work in small groups of no more than four trainees per group. Take a sheet of A3 paper for each group.

- Write the question *Why?* in the centre of your group's sheet.
- Brainstorm together what you think are the key reasons for teaching languages at primary school.
- Note down the benefits that spring to mind.
- After five minutes, share your group's suggestions with the rest of the class.
- Discuss your findings.

## REFLECTIVE TASK

(You will need your Key Stage 2 Framework.)

Open your Framework at Part 2:4. Read the statements on pages 4 and 5.

- How do these reasons match your own suggestions from the brainstorm?
- Are there any new ones which would be useful to note when composing a school's Primary Languages Policy or when advocating languages to your head teacher?

Driscoll (1999) sums up the reasons for Primary Languages teaching and learning as follows:

> *Learning a language is a valuable and worthwhile enterprise at any age because it provides the possibility of practical communication; it is also a source of valuable intellectual stimulation and enjoyment; it cultivates broader perspectives and insights into other cultures and enables people to gain insights into their own culture and language through contrast.*

> (Driscoll, 1999, p2)

Describing the specific context of the primary school, and drawing on the work of Sharpe (1991), she goes on:

> *The primary curriculum provides a wealth of opportunities for the foreign language to be exploited within other primary topics and the memorisation of stock phrases*

*can be connected to the pupils' experience through story telling, songs and play activities which help to generate an enjoyable and motivating environment for foreign language learning...pupils can develop confidence in the family atmosphere and caring culture of the primary school with fellow classmates they know well and with whom they have learnt all manner of basic skills over the years.*

(Driscoll, 1999, p12)

The Key Stage 2 Framework suggests that language learning:

- stimulates children's creativity;
- supports oracy and literacy;
- leads to gains across the curriculum;
- supports and celebrates the international dimension.

It sums up benefits for children through language learning as opportunities to:

- gain enjoyment, pride and a sense of achievement;
- express themselves creatively and imaginatively in another language;
- apply and develop their knowledge of languages and language learning;
- explore and apply strategies to improve their learning;
- explore their own cultural identities and those of others.

The Framework is also described as providing teachers with:

*the freedom to be creative and innovative and to devise programmes of work and activities which will engage, excite and challenge children. The course content should be stimulating, enjoyable and challenging, reflecting children's increasing maturity and offering them inspiration to communicate and use language creatively and imaginatively.*

(DfES, 2005, p5)

# Patterns of provision: different curriculum models

This section outlines the main teaching approaches that have been adopted in primary schools in the UK. There is currently a huge diversity of provision in England, although with each year that the Key Stage 2 Framework and the entitlement are implemented, the programmes are gradually becoming more coherent. Nonetheless, broadly speaking, programmes are sited along a continuum from intensive teaching contexts with fairly complex linguistic content on the one hand, to others in which a much more modest exposure to the FL(s) is offered and the broader educative value of taster experiences of FLs are stressed. As a Primary Languages Co-ordinator, you will need to be aware of the advantages and disadvantages of the various models, so that you can advise your senior management team about what type of provision might be the most appropriate for your specific local setting.

## Language awareness

There has been substantial debate over the role of language awareness work in Primary Languages provision (Poole, 1994; 1995). In a conference presentation Downes describes language awareness as

> *explicit knowledge about language and conscious perception and sensitivity in language learning, language teaching and language use.*

> (Downes, 2002)

For many years Hawkins (1984) argued that a language awareness approach is a means of preparing for language learning, a learning how to learn, providing *education of the ear* (Hawkins, 1987) and a forum for the discussion of language diversity. The child's own language and examples from other languages, provide a basis for comparison, so that language awareness strengthens children's understanding of the structure and concept of language and overall basic literacy can be promoted.

Language awareness on its own has been claimed to allow for better co-ordination from primary to secondary levels, as language learning is intentionally limited to knowledge that will not be viewed as interference upon transfer to secondary school. Because most if not all the discussion takes places in English, language awareness programmes are particularly suited to delivery by the primary teacher, who needs to have little *active* knowledge of a specific foreign language.

Since the 2003–05 Key Stage 2 Pathfinder initiative, some LAs with a mix of children from a range of cultural backgrounds, such as Coventry, have produced language awareness materials. Parallel developments in South Gloucestershire at the International Learning and Research Centre have led to the creation of a series of six units entitled *The Languages Bridge.* Built round a number of core linguistic structures with examples from several languages, these raise children's awareness of the existence of different languages, with the intention of teaching learners how to learn languages and providing the *tools for multilingualism* (Martin, 2006; 2007).

In Cambridgeshire, the Esmée Fairbairn Foundation has since 2004 funded the Association of School and College Leaders' multi-lingual language awareness project (Downes, 2002; 2007; 2008). Downes claims that the language need of English native speakers is diversity, not just one language. Years 5 and 6 of seven primary schools, feeding into four secondary schools, have learned a term each of French, German, Latin, Japanese, Spanish and Punjabi, taught by the class teacher with good quality user-friendly teaching materials which are primary specific. Downes stresses that it is important to choose languages from several 'families' to provide a range of sounds, structures, writing systems and cultures. Examples are Romance, Germanic, Eastern, Indian, African, Eastern European as well as Latin!

In the Key Stage 2 Framework, a language awareness component is partly incorporated into the Knowledge about Language strand (see Chapter 3 and Chapter 7).

## Sensitisation/encounter

Sensitisation programmes (known as *sensibilisation* in France) are designed to develop the confident handling of simple phrases and vocabulary and a broader base line competence in one or more languages. Their aim is to develop children's understanding about language learning by means of an encounter with one and, occasionally, several foreign language(s), with an emphasis on the primary child's present interests and cognitive development. A sensitisation approach can start at any age, including Key Stage 1 and Foundation Stage, and is typically delivered by the primary class teacher, assisted by resources designed with the specific needs of the non-specialist linguist in mind and by INSET, or occasionally, native speaker support. These custom-made packages have an intentionally restricted inventory of language items so as to enable the teacher to present a modest amount of language, which is integrated in varying degrees into the daily life of the primary classroom. Economical as far as curriculum time is concerned, they have appeared well suited to the context in England, where many teachers are constrained by a combination of lack of confidence, training and time. Sensitisation tends to be more within the reach of the retrained primary teacher, as content is less prescribed and the promotion of positive attitudes is prioritised. Children may develop some basic competence and confident handling of a limited number of formulaic phrases, but not to the same extent as in a language competence programme.

As Johnstone notes, an advantage of an encounter/sensitisation approach is that:

> *it gives children actual experience of learning one or more languages rather than simply learning about them as in language awareness. The disadvantage is that, especially where several languages are briefly encountered, there is likely to be insufficient time in which to make substantial progress in any one of them.*
>
> (Johnstone, 1994, p7)

(Compare the National Languages Strategy aspirations that children should reach *a recognized level of competence* at age 11.)

## Language acquisition and language competence

Language acquisition programmes (*apprentissage*) aim to develop a measure of language proficiency in children and enhance their linguistic attainment. Because they emphasise performance and progression, and tend to include the four skills (listening, speaking, reading and writing) they require more curriculum time and are almost inevitably based on the concentrated study of a single language. As such, they place requirements upon the teacher's linguistic knowledge and, until the advent of the National Languages Strategy, tended to be based on a drop-in model with visits by a peripatetic specialist, often from the secondary sector, who taught the foreign language in discrete timetabled time. The approach to instruction is thus an overt one, and the language itself the prime focus of each lesson. Particularly when language competence programmes are offered at primary school, it is essential that secondary schools take account of children's prior learning so that progress in the foreign language is maintained (Martin, 2000a; 2006) (see Chapter 7).

## Embedding/integration

Rixon (1992) makes a distinction between language competence approaches and those which are more holistic. In the former, the new language is timetabled as an additional subject in the curriculum, whereas the holistic approach integrates the new language in a variety of ways into the existing primary curriculum. Embedding is economic in terms of curriculum time, because the new language is used for the purposes of communication through the school day. The MLPS initiative in Scotland adopted an holistic approach based on the five areas of the primary curriculum in Scotland (language arts, environmental studies, mathematics, expressive arts, religious and moral education).

Many holistic models also include a stand-alone component to introduce, practise and reinforce vocabulary and structures in a discrete way.

Certainly, whatever methods are adopted, it is vital to reinforce the new language throughout the school day by including it within daily routines (although this can only really happen when the primary teacher is the language teacher).

Elements of the new language can also permeate other subject areas, such as mathematics, geography, PE, music, art. Several writers (Bell, 1996; Tierney and Hope, 1998; Muir, 1999) show that doing so promotes real communication throughout the school day and permits children to make connections between the concepts about the world which they are learning about in the rest of the curriculum and the new language.

Embedding and integration are weak versions of Content and Language Integrated Learning (CLIL) and immersion (see below).

We should note that whatever model a school chooses initially, the realities and vicissitudes of local context, such as the continuing availability of suitably qualified teachers, are likely to cause shifts in the specification of provision, and this is one of the issues related to sustainability and building capacity – the need to train and maintain a suitably qualified workforce in Primary Languages. Sustainability – a school's capacity to continue to staff and resource a Primary Languages programme over time – is considered further in Chapter 8 (see page 127).

As we saw above, sensitisation models tend to stress motivational and attitudinal aspects of language learning, together with limited use of the new language. Sometimes children move on from sensitisation in, say, Years 3 and 4 to language competence style work in the upper stages of Key Stage 2. Language competence and language sensitisation are both ways of initiating children into foreign language learning, although with a different emphasis, and both may incorporate an element of language awareness work, although until the advent of the Key Stage 2 Framework, this occurred infrequently (Martin, 2000a; 2000b).

As you will see in the next chapter, the Key Stage 2 Framework, while being non-statutory, nonetheless promotes a language acquisition/competence model. Indeed, if you turn to Part 2:49 you will see that the Framework makes no assumption about there being just one way of organising teaching and learning of languages. Intentionally, it supports a range of organisational models stating:

- *Some schools may wish to offer a single language taught across four years, often in collaboration with a secondary school.*
- *Some schools wish to offer experience of a range of different languages, developing knowledge about language and language learning strategies, in the early stages and concentrating on a single language later in the learning process.*
- *Some schools have adopted a two-language model.*

(DfES, 2005, Part 2, p49)

**REFLECTIVE TASK**

Based on your observations and experiences in schools so far, what kinds of models of provision have you encountered?

● Are all children in Key Stage 2 having a consistent experience of language learning or are some classes more geared towards language awareness or sensitisation and others to language competence?

● How are schools with which you are familiar delivering Primary Languages?

Share your observations with your peers.

Two other approaches should be briefly mentioned, although they are much rarer in the UK context.

# Content and Language Integrated Learning (CLIL)

The Nuffield Languages Inquiry (2000) recommended that there should be a programme of bilingual learning, with new content being learned through the medium of the FL. In September 2002, the Content and Language Integration Project (CLIP) was piloted in eight schools and seeks to raise standards of attainment across the curriculum. Lord Dearing's Review of the 14–19 curriculum suggested the implementation of Content and Language Integrated Learning (CLIL) projects, and in 2007 the TDA initiated several CLIL pilots in both primary and secondary schools, and some of you may be involved in these through your HEI.

CLIL and CLIP approaches have links with a much more substantial experience of language learning, currently rare in the UK, called immersion.

# Immersion

In immersion classes, not only are aspects of the curriculum taught through the medium of the foreign language, but teachers are typically native speakers, or at least fluent speakers of the language in question. A good deal of the evidence from immersion learning comes from Canada, where English children are learning French. Actually there are different forms of immersion, in which the intensity varies: in some total immersion programmes, all subjects are taught through the FL, in partial immersion, only some subjects. Immersion can start with different age groups of children, so some programmes may be early immersion and others late immersion, and these can also be combined, i.e. early total, or late partial. In the UK, a well-known instance is Walker Road School in Scotland.

The following chapters will help you consider practical ways of delivering high quality teaching.

A SUMMARY OF **KEY POINTS**

> **We need to bear in mind the context in which language learning is taking place.**

> **Younger learners are better at imitating and if well taught, can pronounce the new language accurately.**

> **This ability to mimic has repercussions for us as teachers, who must provide high quality pronunciation models and access to native speaker voices.**

> Starting earlier provides children with more time for language learning.
> There are several benefits to starting language learning younger.
> Decisions have to be made about models of provision, and schools need to be clear about the implications of language awareness, sensitisation and language competence programmes for course content, staffing and outcomes.

**MOVING** *ON* > > > > > > MOVING *ON* > > > > > > MOVING *ON*

The benefits of an early start to language learning are potentially enormous but depend, as we have seen, on high quality teaching and learning opportunities. Look for training events both in the UK and abroad (see Chapter 9) to help you become an excellent practitioner and in particular to improve your own linguistic skills. Even as a teacher trainee, you may be able to attend some of your Early Language Learning Regional Support Group meetings (see NACELL website below for details of location and sessions).

**FURTHER READING** FURTHER READING **FURTHER READING** FURTHER READING

CILT/DfES (2004) *Piece by piece. Languages in primary schools. Twelve questions you may want to ask.* London: CILT. This booklet has a page of sources of information and support with key addresses and websites available at www.nacell.org.uk/cdrom/questions.pdf.

Driscoll, P. and Frost, D. (eds) (1999) *The teaching of modern foreign languages in the primary school.* London: Routledge.

Johnstone, R. (1994) *Teaching modern languages in the primary school.* Scottish Council for Research in Education.

Jones, J. and Coffey, S. (2006) *Modern foreign languages 5–11.* London: David Fulton Publishers.

Sharpe, K. (2001) *Modern foreign languages in the primary school. The what, why and how of early MFL teaching.* London: Kogan Page.

## Useful websites

www.cilt.org.uk – for all information about CILT, The National Centre for Languages
www.nacell.org.uk – National Advisory Centre on Early Language Learning
NACELL is being brought together with the Primary Languages Training Zone site, and eventually both NACELL and the Training Zone will be accessed through www.primarylanguages.org.uk
http://www.standards.dcsf.gov.uk/primary/features/learning_teaching/landt_cpd – *Excellence and Enjoyment: learning and teaching in the primary years*

# 3
# Finding your way around the Key Stage 2 Framework for Languages

By the end of this chapter you will have:

- become familiar with the three parts of the Framework and practised navigating around the document, identifying the specific learning objectives and investigating the strands;
- considered some Framework exemplification models from the Primary Languages Training Zone.

This chapter addresses the following Professional Standards for QTS:
Q3a, Q3b, Q7a

## What is the Key Stage 2 Framework for Languages?

At the time of writing, Primary Languages are still a new curriculum area for most schools and many senior managers are relying on subject specialists to guide them through this initiative and to help them to manage the changes as it is implemented. As a newly qualified specialist you will need to know, at least, where to find specific Framework content, so that you can point colleagues in the right direction.

The Key Stage 2 Framework for Languages was created to support the Government's National Languages Strategy, which, as we saw in Chapter 1, made a commitment to the introduction of an entitlement to language learning for every child throughout Key Stage 2 by 2010. It is a:

> core document, offering a practical reference tool for planning, teaching and monitoring the learning process. The Framework is designed to support primary school teachers in building their own courses.
>
> (DfES, 2005, Part 1 p3)

Another relevant national initiative is *Excellence and enjoyment: A strategy for primary schools* (DfES, 2003a), which suggests a freeing up of previous requirements and encourages breadth and balance in the curriculum. It thus allows for the inclusion of Primary Languages as a new subject and fits nicely with the embedding models of provision which we discussed in Chapter 2. The holistic approach and encouragement to exploit creativity and cross-curricular links, provide:

> ... a natural support for the primary MFL entitlement: teachers will be encouraged to introduce primary MFL not as a bolt-on extra, but as an integrated part of a rich and coherent curriculum. It will be a means of reinforcing and extending work on literacy, and a subject with natural links across the curriculum that can be

exploited to enhance pupils' overall learning experiences. Primary Strategy colleagues are closely involved with the development of the MFL Framework document and we are committed to ensuring that the two strategies are mutually supportive.

(www.standards.dfes.gov.uk/primary/features/literacy/939697/
DCFS Standards site: Key Stage 2 Framework for modern languages, March 2004)

In order to design Parts 1 and 2 of the Key Stage 2 Framework for Languages, the following documents were also drawn upon:

- the objectives for English, PSHE, geography, history, art and design, music and ICT as set out in the National Curriculum Programmes of Study for Key Stages 1 and 2;
- the National Literacy Strategy (DfEE, 1998);
- the National Numeracy Strategy (DfEE, 1999);
- National Curriculum non-statutory guidelines for MFL at Key Stage 2 (DfEE/QCA, 1999a);
- original QCA Schemes of Work for Modern Foreign Languages at Key Stage 2 (QCA 2000);
- Speaking, Listening, Learning: working with children in Key Stages 1 and 2 (Primary National Strategy and QCA, 2003).

Part 3, published in 2007, refers to more recent documentation such as the new QCA Schemes of Work (QCA, 2007) and *Every Child Matters* (DfES, 2004), with its aim that every child should have the support they need to be healthy, stay safe, enjoy and achieve, make a positive contribution and achieve economic well being. As the Council for Subject Associations affirms in its publication *Primary Subjects*.

*Teaching languages in primary school provides rich opportunities to make every child matter – through celebrating linguistic diversity and valuing every child's cultural and linguistic background. Children are encouraged to make a positive contribution to the community by respecting others and working collaboratively; they also develop team skills, which will contribute to their future economic well being.*

(CfSA, 2008, p1)

# A climbing frame, not a cage

The Framework is intended to be a trellis to support learning rather than a means of restricting teachers, a *climbing frame, not a cage* (DfES, 2005, Part 1 p4). It recognises that schools will be beginning from many different starting points. The Framework needs to be comprehensive and as applicable to those schools already engaged in Primary Languages with an established programme as to those with no previous experience, and to all the permutations of practice and context in between.

The Key Stage 2 Framework for Languages may seem a daunting document at first glance: it is nearly 300 pages long. However, it is important to note that the Framework is designed to be introduced over time. It is there to support what is already happening in Primary Languages and to underpin capacity building over a period of years as an experienced workforce is gradually established.

# Becoming familiar with the Framework

In this section we shall be looking more closely at the layout, content and organisation of the Framework.

## The three parts

The Key Stage 2 Framework comes in three parts. As a first step, you need to be sure about what each part contains. You will find that effort spent familiarising yourself with the different emphases of each section and where to find guidance on specific issues will repay the investment in time saved later.

Each Part (1, 2 and 3) is numbered in the following way:

- Part 1 pages 1–90;
- Part 2 pages 1–71;
- Part 3 pages 1–136.

(The numbers are not continuous throughout all three parts, each Part begins again). The three Parts are indicated by their colour-coded dividers, which mark out each of the sections. Part 1 has sea-green dividers, plus some brightly coloured dividers for each of the Year groups 3–6. Part 2 has mid-blue section dividers and Part 3 a pale bluey-grey.

**PRACTICAL TASK** PRACTICAL TASK PRACTICAL TASK PRACTICAL TASK PRACTICAL TASK

(You will need your Key Stage 2 Framework.)

Open any page of the Key Stage 2 Framework. On each page, in the **top right-hand corner**, the number between the quotation marks, 'one', 'two', is the number of the section: and **is printed in the same colour as the section dividers**. These coloured numbers show which section or part of the Framework you are in. In the **bottom right-hand corner** in the footer on each page is a description of the section, whose number appears at the top of the same page, plus a page number i.e. *The Key Stage 2 Framework for Languages – Introduction* or *The Key Stage 2 Framework for Languages – Progression by strand*. It helps to know this if you need to remove (and replace) any pages for planning purposes.

### Part 1

Part 1 is the Framework itself. The introduction demonstrates the value placed on a serious approach to raising the nation's languages capability. It sets out an overview of the rationale for the Framework, including snapshots from the results of surveys on the attitudes of children learning languages in primary school.

If you are a trainee **not** intending to be a subject leader, or a teacher working just with your own class, **Part 1 is the most important part of the Framework for you to get to know, because it includes the learning objectives for each of the four years of Key Stage 2, as well as teaching activities.**

Let us now try to find our way round the Key Stage 2 Framework. **For all the following tasks you will need your Framework to hand.**

**PRACTICAL TASK** PRACTICAL TASK PRACTICAL TASK PRACTICAL TASK PRACTICAL TASK

**What's in Part 1?**

Table 3.1 on page 25 contains the main headings from the Part 1 contents page, indicating the seven sections which make up Part 1. Create a table like this for yourself.

● Using the sea-green section dividers for Part 1, list what you would find in each section. You can use the subheadings in the box below and cross off each one as you find where it is located in Part 1. Read the sub headings through carefully and fill them in on the right-hand side of the table, so that you have a complete overview of the contents in Part 1. Some are done for you, to help you get started.

Subheadings:

> Year 4 teaching activities
> The National Languages strategy
> Year 6 at a glance
> Overview of the learning objectives
> Oracy, Literacy, Intercultural Understanding, Knowledge about Language, Language Learning Strategies.
> What do children in Year 3 think about language learning?
> Message from the Education Minister
> The Framework as a point of reference
> Year 6 teaching activities
> What do children in Year 6 think about language learning?
> Year 4 at a glance
> Structure of the Framework
> Year 3/Year 4/Year 5/Year 6 Expectations
> Learning objectives
> Year 3/Year 4/Year 5/Year 6 Outcomes
> Year 3 teaching activities
> Year 5 teaching activities
> What do children in Year 4 think about language learning?
> Year 3 at a glance
> What do children in Year 5 think about language learning?

## Getting to know the Key Stage 2 Framework task

Remove the coloured section dividers with numbered tabs. Place the ringbinder to one side. Concentrating on the contents pages and section information, try the following activity to help you familiarise yourself with the KS2 Framework as a document and answer the following question. *What's in the Framework?*

### What's in the Framework? Getting to know Part 1

The grid below shows on the left hand side the section numbers and against each one a corresponding section title. Using the additional information on the individual section dividers, write into the grid against the appropriate section number, what you would find in each section of Part one. The first example is partly completed for you!

**Table 3.1 Key Stage 2 Framework, Part 1**

| | KS2 Framework for Languages Part 1 | |
|---|---|---|
| **Section number** | **Contents page heading** | **Further information on section contents from divider** |
| | **Foreword** | |
| 1 | Introduction | *The National Languages Strategy* |
| | | *Overview of the Learning Objectives* |
| 2 | **Using the Learning Objectives** | |
| 3 | **Year 3** | |
| | | *Learning Objectives* |
| 4 | Year 4 | *Expectations and Outcomes* |
| 5 | Year 5 | |
| | | *Year 5 – Teaching Activities* |
| 6 | Year 6 | |
| 7 | **Progression by strand** | |

You now have a list of what you can find in Part 1. In order to begin to familiarise yourself with some of the detail, turn to the four A3 fold-out double page spreads entitled *At a Glance,* one for each of Years 3–6 (on pages 19, 33, 45, 57 of Part 1).

You will find these really helpful, because they give you an overview of a whole year's objectives all on one page. These pages help you see how the different strands are linked to each other. It is noteworthy that:

> The strands are interconnected and support each other; they would rarely be taught in isolation.

> (DfES, 2005, Part 1, p9)

**PRACTICAL TASK** PRACTICAL TASK PRACTICAL TASK PRACTICAL TASK PRACTICAL TASK

Getting an overview of the learning objectives

Read the four *At a Glance* overview pages for each of Years 3, 4, 5, 6 (Part 1, pages 19, 33, 45, 57).

- What *features* do each of the years have *in common*?

- *How many* strands are there?
- What are they *called?*
- Which do you think are the *core strands*, which provide the Framework?
- In what *language* are the learning objectives expressed?
- *Why* do you think this is?

Share what you have discovered with other trainees.

Through doing the above task, you should have discovered several important facts about the Key Stage 2 Framework for Languages and especially the contents of Part 1, i.e. that the Framework is:

- generic (can be applied to any language);
- content-free (there are not any prescribed topics);
- skills-based;
- made up of five strands;
- a structured means of support to planning through the objectives;
- written especially for primary teachers, who may be non-specialist linguists (although of course it is very helpful for other readers too);
- a national point of reference as it is freely available to all schools;
- meant to be used flexibly and adapted to local circumstances so that it works for you.

*The learning objectives*

Three learning objectives are core strands which focus on:

- oracy;
- literacy;
- intercultural understanding;

for each of the four years of Key Stage 2 with expected **outcomes** for children at specific ages. They will help you decide what to teach in each year.

**Oracy** relates to the skills of speaking and listening, and **Literacy** to reading and writing. In practice oracy and literacy are interrelated and you will need to present your children with a balance of appropriate speaking, listening, reading and writing opportunities throughout Key Stage 2. This will depend on individual children's abilities and you should accommodate the children in your classes according to their needs, differentiating tasks so that children are included appropriately.

**Intercultural Understanding** emphasises finding out about the cultural contexts of the language being learned, as well as children's own cultural background, so that they come to accept, appreciate and celebrate difference.

> *The teaching of primary languages makes a valuable contribution to the* Every Child Matters *agenda by introducing children to the languages and cultures of others. It helps create a situation in which children learn to respect the diversity of the society and of the world in which we live. They can with confidence and security develop a curiosity about languages and language learning. When learning a new language, children are encouraged to reflect upon their own*

languages and cultures. The primary classroom provides an ideal setting in which to tackle sensitive and fundamental issues of identity and self-esteem, beliefs and traditions – all of which are part of the rich arena of primary languages teaching and learning.

(DCSF, 2007, Part 3, p1)

You will also find two **cross-cutting** strands:

- Knowledge about Language (KAL);
- Language Learning Strategies (LLS).

KAL is concerned with how language works and so deals with aspects of language awareness (see Chapter 2) and also the lexis and structure of both the new language and how it is similar to and different from English (and to some extent, other languages). We shall be considering KAL in Chapter 7.

LLS are to do with teaching children how to learn and are associated with research, which began in the 1970s, into what makes the *good language learner* (Naiman et al., 1978). Naiman's work was based on that of Stern (1975) who described what 'good' language learners appear to do, which less successful language learners do not. Initially this area of research mainly focused on adult learners of English but more recently it has turned to modern language teaching in school-based contexts. Grenfell (2007) makes the point that rather than the *teacher teaching the language* there has been a shift towards *creating the conditions for the **learner to learn**.* Language learner strategies offer the tools for learners to manage their own learning (Grenfell and Erler, 2007). We shall consider language learning/ learner strategies again in Chapter 7 when we are discussing progression.

## REFLECTIVE TASK

### Beginning to understand the learning objectives

In order to gain a 'feel' for these five strands, open the Framework Part 1 on pages 7–9 where you will find some summary descriptions of each strand. (It would be helpful if your tutor were to copy each of the five summaries onto separate colour cards.) If there are sufficient numbers, we suggest you work in groups of five, and each of you takes one paragraph or one card.

- Take **one each of the cards** (or focus on **one summary** only to start with).
- Sum up in two or three bullet points the key statements made in the description of your strand.
- If you are looking at **Oracy**, also consider the following question: The Framework states that children must be given regular opportunities to listen to good models of pronunciation. What can we do to ensure that children do receive excellent models?
- If your strand is **Literacy**, can you think of actual examples of different forms of text which children would enjoy reading?
- **Intercultural Understanding**: The summary suggests that there are opportunities to link Intercultural understanding to work in other curriculum areas. Share examples of how this might be done.
- **Knowledge about Language**: What kind of structural patterns might you need to make children aware of in the language you are intending to teach?
- **Language Learning Strategies**: What does your group understand by the term Language Learning Strategies?

The Framework gives sample teaching activities for each of the objectives by year and makes connections between the strands. In addition, Oracy, Literacy and Intercultural Understanding are listed separately by strand to help you monitor progress. In order to be inclusive, references are made to approaches you can adopt to ensure all children are included.

---

**PRACTICAL TASK** PRACTICAL TASK PRACTICAL TASK PRACTICAL TASK PRACTICAL TASK

**Expectations and Outcomes**

(For this task you will need the four pages which set out the Expectations and Outcomes for Years 3, 4, 5 and 6. It might be helpful to **lift out pages 18, 32, 44 and 56** to save having to keep turning the pages in the ring binder.)

You will see that each of these four pages is divided into two columns. On the left are the **Expectations**, which summarise the expectations for learning and teaching for a particular year, and on the right the **Outcomes** column, which sets out what children are expected **to be able to do** at the **end** of each **year**. (These four pages will be useful to discuss with colleagues and head teachers if they ask you about what is expected of children learning Primary Languages.)

- With a highlighter, carefully mark the key steps which children will be taking in each of the strands.

- For the Oracy strand, you will see they move from the familiar to less familiar, from responding in chorus as a whole class to responding individually. What other steps can you trace?

- Note these down and share your findings with the rest of your group.

---

## Part 2

If you intend to become a Subject Leader for Primary Languages in your school, you need to be familiar with the contents of *Part 2 Guidance on Implementation,* which is for head teachers, managers, and curriculum leaders. We shall be considering Part 2 in more detail in Chapters 7 and 9 on transition and subject leadership.

**Part 2** is divided into five sections. As it might be consulted separately from Part 1, by managers less concerned with the detail of lesson planning, general information about the Framework and the National Languages Strategy are repeated. The contents are:

1. **Primary Language Learning** – an introduction to the Framework for all users;
2. **Co-ordinating provision** – Advice for head teachers, senior managers and subject co-ordinators;
3. **Getting started** – Advice for primary schools and teachers introducing languages for the first time;
4. **Moving on** – Advice for primary schools and teachers already teaching languages;
5. **Supporting primary entitlement** – Advice for secondary schools.

## Part 3

Published in 2007, **Part 3, Planning for Entitlement** is a practical tool to help implement decisions about Primary Languages. Primary Languages Co-ordinators will find Part 3 very relevant on account of the detailed exemplar material. If you are a class teacher, you will find it useful to dip into to answer specific questions.

As well as the planning tools, there are detailed examples of how to embed language learning using cross-curricular links. There is advice on:

- planning for progression over four years;
- planning a multilingual approach;
- managing mixed age classes;
- addressing the challenges faced by small rural schools;
- record keeping and assessment;
- supporting continuity and transition from Key Stage 2 to Key Stage 3;
- meeting the needs of all children, including those with English as an additional language.

The third part of the Framework has been divided into eight sections, organised under the following headings on the contents page:

1. **A flying start** – using the Framework as a planning tool;
2. **Seeing the whole picture** – planning;
3. **Making the links** – integrating languages with the rest of the curriculum;
4. **Inclusion** – languages for all;
5. **Leaps and bounds** – progression;
6. **Building on achievement** – transition and continuity;
7. **Celebrating achievement** – assessment and recording;
8. **Working together** – using the Framework in different contexts.

These themes will be touched upon throughout this book. So, for example, if you are intending to become a Primary Languages Co-ordinator, the strategic overview for long- and medium-term planning will be especially useful. If you are aiming just to teach your class, you will benefit from the sample short-term plans. The latter are particularly helpful as they include a large number of different ideas for teaching activities. Why not consider duplicating them for colleagues who need a reminder of a repertoire of quick and easy teaching strategies?

---

**PRACTICAL TASK** PRACTICAL TASK PRACTICAL TASK PRACTICAL TASK PRACTICAL TASK

**What's in the Key Stage 2 Framework, Part 3**

Using the pale blue **contents page** and **section information** on the dividers from the Key Stage 2 Framework Part 3, where would you look for information on the following? Write in column 2 the section number and pages to which you would refer. An example is done for you.

| Issue | Part 3: section/ pages |
| --- | --- |
| We need to find online links | Part 3:1, p5 |
| We wish to challenge able learners | |
| We intend to employ an FLA as support | |
| We'd like to know the QCA view on progression in Primary Languages | |
| Our school is considering the European Language Portfolio | |
| We want to link our Primary Languages with other curriculum areas | |
| Our EAL children need support | |

---

# How the learning objectives work in practice: A first look at the Primary Languages Training Zone

Working with teachers in the primary classroom, the Primary Languages website (www.primarylanguages.org.uk) has been developed by CILT, and presents examples of the Framework in action. It shows how the five strands can inform teaching and learning and underpin progression across the four years of Key Stage 2. It offers comprehensive access to professional development for you, now as a trainee, and in the future, as a newly qualified and, later, experienced teacher.

The examples on the website are regularly updated. You can save the material in My Zone to help you plan your lessons.

Each example comes with a **language file** and a **transcript** to help you become more confident. You can download language files to your iPod or computer and improve your language skills (find out more about this facility on the Language support page). There are also *think pieces* to help you explore key issues and develop your practice. You can print off these and use them personally now. Later in your career you will find them useful for whole school training or to support staff development in small groups.

In this section we shall consider some exemplification of the core strands of the Key Stage 2 Framework. From the home page, you will see that the Training Zone is divided into three parts: for Leaders, Teachers and Trainers. The NACELL website and the Primary Languages site are being combined into a single site which is planned to go live at the Primary Languages Show in 2009.

## Oracy

**PRACTICAL TASK** PRACTICAL TASK PRACTICAL TASK PRACTICAL TASK PRACTICAL TASK

Select Using the Key Stage 2 Framework and you will hear a teacher talking about how she uses the flexibility of the Framework to fit some of her language work into the topic of the cafe as part of the design and technology curriculum.

Let's look at the first Framework Learning Objective: **Oracy**, which combines listening and speaking. You will see that the 'Using the Key Stage 2 Framework' strand is divided in five sub themes, of which Oracy is the first.

● Read the summary about Oracy next to the video clip on the right hand side. How does this link to the description of Oracy that you looked at in the Practical Task on page 25 and the Oracy objectives on the *At a Glance* pages?

Currently there are 12 sets of activities related to the sub-theme: Oracy. They are:

● Animal parts (Spanish);
● Flashcards – planets (French);
● Animal parts game (Spanish);
● Clothes game (Spanish);

- Clothes (Spanish);
- Flag game (French);
- Conversation performance (German);
- Greetings (French);
- Objects (French);
- Conversation model (German);
- Colours practice (Chinese);
- Helicopters presentation (French).

---

**PRACTICAL TASK** PRACTICAL TASK PRACTICAL TASK PRACTICAL TASK PRACTICAL TASK

**Oracy – Flag game (French)**

In this game, the children are trying to find a *Tricolore* flag hidden behind some coloured circles on the Smartboard. Watch the video clip.

- What do children have to be able to do in order to play the game?
- What Oracy objectives is the activity meeting? Check your answers against the commentary provided with the video clip (click on Professional Development).
- Can you make any links with the objectives for Intercultural Understanding? If so, which ones?

---

# Literacy

Now let us consider **Literacy** (reading and writing).

You will need to follow the same procedure as above for Oracy, except that this time you select Literacy as the sub-theme. At the time of writing there are nine sets of activities related to the sub-theme Literacy. They are:

- Sound game;
- Compound sentences (French);
- Matching envelopes;
- Gap filling;
- Planets story (French);
- Writing colours (French);
- Sound/spelling story;
- Read a poem;
- Vowels (French).

---

**PRACTICAL TASK** PRACTICAL TASK PRACTICAL TASK PRACTICAL TASK PRACTICAL TASK

**Literacy – Writing colours (French)**

This video clip shows how the teacher is building on the work done in Oracy, in order to develop literacy skills. Watch carefully and consider ways the teacher is enabling children to practise writing the colours which they have already learned orally.

- How does she sequence the process?
- How is the teacher making sound and spelling links?
- What kind of features is she drawing children's attention to?

- Can you spot how she is developing simple KAL and LLS?
- How does she respond to a slip in pronunciation from one of the pairs?

Both the Oracy and Literacy extracts which we have considered indicate the way in which listening, speaking, reading and writing are linked and also used for a purpose. We shall look at addressing these two strands in greater detail in Chapter 4.

# Intercultural Understanding

We shall explore Intercultural Understanding in more detail in Chapter 6. For this sub-theme, there are presently six video clips.

- Chocolate cakes (Spanish).
- Traditional flower song (Chinese).
- Easter words (German).
- Penfriend letter (French).
- Harvest market assembly (French).
- International exchange (Year 2 French).

Aspects of Intercultural Understanding can be taught and celebrated in and out of lessons. In this extract we see a head teacher leading an assembly on the topic of a market in France which some children had recently visited.

---

**PRACTICAL TASK** PRACTICAL TASK PRACTICAL TASK PRACTICAL TASK PRACTICAL TASK

**Intercultural Understanding – Harvest market**

Go to Key Stage 2 Framework and the sub-theme Intercultural Understanding and select Harvest Market.

- What differences which they noticed do children mention?
- If you were one of the class teachers, how would you build on this assembly with your class?
- This discussion is taking place in English. Is there a small amount of key language which you could share with your children in French?
- If your language is other than French, would it be possible to devise an assembly on a harvest theme or similar celebration?
- How might you do so and what features would you discuss – even if children had not visited the country concerned?

---

A SUMMARY OF **KEY POINTS**

> The Key Stage 2 Framework for Languages was developed to provide practical support and guidance to teachers, schools and LAs. It is a flexible document designed to be adapted to a variety of circum- stances.

> The three parts are written for different audiences and users. The generic learning objectives are found in Part 1 and further exemplification of planning using the learning objectives in Part 3. Both these parts are really practical and useful for primary class teachers as well as subject leaders.

> **Part 2 is aimed at managers, head teachers and secondary colleagues and is helpful for subject leaders as it deals with more strategic decisions about implementation.**

## MOVING *ON* > > > > > > MOVING *ON* > > > > > > MOVING *ON*

You should now be in a position to begin to use the Framework more confidently to help you as you plan. If you aspire to become a Primary Languages Co-ordinator, you need to work with all three parts. If you are intending to be a classroom teacher of languages, you should focus on Parts 1 and 3, and adapt the ideas for planning for your children's needs.

## FURTHER READING FURTHER READING FURTHER READING FURTHER READING

DfES (2005) *The Key Stage 2 Framework for Languages*. Nottingham: DfES publications. This provides you with Parts 1 and 2.

DCSF (2007) *The Key Stage 2 Framework for Languages*. Nottingham: DCSF publications. This provides you with Part 3.

# Useful websites

www.teachernet.gov.uk/publications Download or order copies, using reference 1721-2005DCD-EN for Parts 1 and 2, 00171-2007DOM-EN for Part 3

www.primarylanguages.org.uk – the Primary Languages Training Zone has a wealth of practical exemplification from the Framework

# 4

# Addressing the Oracy
# and Literacy strands

By the end of this chapter you will have:

- investigated the Oracy and Literacy strands of the Key Stage 2 Framework;
- understood how rhymes, songs, stories and physical responses can lead into speaking;
- considered a variety of techniques for presenting and practising new language;
- practised devising a staged question and answer series;
- prepared to plan and deliver a 10–15 minute session in the language of your choice;
- appreciated the need to explicitly teach grapheme–phoneme correspondences (GPCs);
- begun to explore ways of encouraging children to write in the new language;
- become aware of the need to provide opportunities for creative free writing.

This chapter addresses the following Professional Standards for QTS:

**Q7a, Q8, Q10, Q14, Q15**

This chapter considers developing oracy and literacy skills based on the first two strands of the Key Stage 2 Framework. When you start thinking about assessing children's learning in Primary Languages, you will find that the four skills of listening, speaking, reading and writing are separated out. However, as we shall find out in the chapter on progression, the 'four skills' model is, in some respects, outdated. As Mitchell writes:

> In performing real world tasks, skills are typically integrated *for the achievement of some non-language goal, such as reading in order to write.*
>
> (2003, p17 [my emphasis])

The Framework itself states that:

> These broad areas [oracy and literacy] are separated out for planning and monitoring purposes. In the classroom they will invariably be linked and mutually supportive.
>
> (DfES, 2005, Part 1, p6) [my emphasis])

It is therefore noteworthy that rather than a division into listening, speaking, reading and writing, listening and speaking are combined into an Oracy strand, and reading and writing into a Literacy strand, and that both objectives and activities indicate ways of teaching them holistically.

Consider how you can teach skills in combination with each other.

Before we investigate some approaches to addressing the Oracy and Literacy objectives we consider briefly children's different learning styles.

# Learning modalities: visual, auditory and kinaesthetic learners

You will be studying these learning styles in more depth elsewhere in your course. However, in simple terms, let us remind ourselves of the following:

- **Visual learners** are helped most when they can see a visual equivalent of an item: pictures are important but so is seeing the *words.* They respond to decoration and display and little handouts which they can stick in their books.
- **Auditory learners** prefer to learn mainly through hearing and talking. They learn best when involved in talking about something or when the teacher explains verbally. They like reading aloud to themselves, perhaps under their breath rather than completely silently.
- **Kinaesthetic learners** like to get physically involved in the learning process. They learn best by being active, or by making or doing things.

**REFLECTIVE TASK**

Think carefully about how best to provide children with opportunities to learn through all the senses.

# Developing listening, speaking, reading and writing

When we come to introduce children to new language items, the sequencing of activities requires careful thought. Let us look at ways of **presenting and practising** new language.

**REFLECTIVE TASK**

(You need your Key Stage 2 Framework Part 3 and your *At a Glance* page for Year 3.)

To get a feel for the kinds of activities children might engage in, look at Part 3:2 page 19, where you will find an example of a short 15-minute teaching sequence for beginners.

- Read through the suggested sequence and highlight the different steps teacher and children are taking.
- What do you notice about the steps in the teaching and learning sequence?
- What is supporting the teacher and what are children doing at each point?

Let us reflect on the teaching and learning sequence which is for O3.1 *listen and respond to simple rhymes, stories and songs* and O3.2 *recognise and respond to sound patterns and words.*

The sequence starts with presentation of the new language within the context of a little rhyme, song or story. The important thing here is that the language is being introduced not in a vacuum as separate words or lists of nouns, but within the framework of meaningful text. You can present a rhyme or sing yourself, or use a CD with a native speaker voice. This helps to familiarise children with the rhythms and sounds of the new language and gets them used to the intonation patterns. Bearing in mind our note above about meeting different learning styles, why does the sequence suggest mimes and actions? You need to keep eyes and ears open for finger and action rhymes, which by their very nature already lend themselves to physical responses. Alternatively, find or create some clear visuals or use objects themselves as props (secondary MFL colleagues call these realia). Authentic CDs can often be used for listening and responding activities, and also for background music while children are quietly working at other tasks. (See note in Part 2:3, p50 on resources to support oracy and also the double page fold out with details from Four short lessons on *Where in the world*, Part 3:2, p21, to see how this works out in practice.)

What are children doing the very first time the new language is introduced? When the language is presented a second time what do they do? Does it matter that things occur in this order?

There are two points here. The first is what Hawkins (1987; 1996) has termed the *education of the ear,* the importance of providing children with opportunities to hear and absorb the sounds of the new language *before* being asked to produce them aloud for themselves. Secondly, Krashen (1984) called this time of receptive silence, the *silent period*. We can provide this by encouraging children to listen and respond – but initially through actions only. Under O3.1 children are described as *performing* finger rhymes... a statement implying that they may not be saying all the words to begin with but may be joining in by watching and copying the actions only.

Look at the steps in the sequence, which you have highlighted. You will see there are a number of possible physical responses as well as mimes to go with a rhyme or story. The sequence in Part 3, p19 suggests that children might pick up objects (*trouvez*) or point at pictures (*indiquez*). Total physical response to aural input can also include showing (*montrez-moi*) holding up an item or visual.

With beginner learners, whether in Year 3 or earlier, you may simply want children to join in with actions while enjoying a rhyme, song or simple story. Sometimes rhymes and songs will have particular words repeated throughout, and you can invite children to pass an object such as a soft toy round the circle or along the row, or clap, pat their heads or touch their noses, when they hear a specific word or words. Each word can have a different action.

---

**PRACTICAL TASK** PRACTICAL TASK PRACTICAL TASK PRACTICAL TASK PRACTICAL TASK

**Rhymes and songs**

This will work best if you ask your fellow trainees to be the 'children' and do the rhyme or song as you demonstrate it, listening for the chosen items.

Find a finger or action rhyme or song in your chosen language which you could use with Year 3 children and which enables you to focus on a particular word.

- Invent some physical responses to go with your chosen stimulus.

- Bring these examples to a session on developing oracy and share your suggestions for both the songs and the words you would ask children to listen out for.
- Which rhymes and songs are the most appropriate and why?
- What kinds of actions can children do in order to listen and respond?

The kinaesthetic response of doing an action when children recognise a particular word supports different learning styles. Providing lots of opportunities to respond by doing, miming, acting out, holding something up or passing a toy along the row, enables children to show you that they understand but without the pressure to respond verbally immediately. Many children will be eager to say the new words too, but there will be some who will first benefit from a safe environment, where they do not have to speak the new language, until they are ready. Remember, Primary Languages is inclusive of all children.

When you wish children to sing along themselves, select authentic song CDs with care. If they are originally made for native speaker children, they may include language and expressions sung very fast for a beginner learner in an English classroom, quite apart from some of the tunes being unfamiliar and tricky to learn. In order to provide variety and help children access songs in the new language, a good starting point is to take a rhyme, such as 'Two Little Dicky Birds', which children already know in English, and translate it into the new language, with actions. You will find examples of more than 50 finger and action rhymes in French and German in Martin (2002) and a useful list of simple tunes well known to children, to which you can put FL words, in Martin with Cheater (1998). Home-made rhymes and songs of this kind need to be integrated in a balanced way with traditional rhymes and songs for native speaker children to provide variety and good models of pronunciation.

Returning to Part 3:2 p19, you will see that the teacher models key words or phrases from the rhyme, story or song and children demonstrate that they understand by doing the corresponding mime or action. Throughout this part of the sequence they are not being required to make the new sounds themselves, although some may well be doing so! When children know the required actions well, they can play a game by performing the actions and getting you, the teacher, to say the language.

It is only at this point that children and teacher move into the repetition stage, when the key language is modelled once more and children are invited to repeat as well as doing the actions. Then the game is reversed by the teacher miming and children saying the words. Try this out for yourselves as a group with some of you playing the part of the teacher and others the children. This will help you appreciate which of these two versions of the game is easier for the learner.

At the end of the proposed teaching sequence it is suggested that children play the miming and guessing game in pairs. Pairwork of this kind has the advantage of enabling all children to participate, but in a different kind of way from whole class interaction with the teacher. They can swap roles with each other, so that one is miming and the other guessing, and also change partners, so that they are not always listening and speaking to the same child.

With many songs and stories, this is where you will want to leave it. Do not try to squeeze too much out of songs, stories and rhymes. Children need to really enjoy working with little texts, having fun and learning some language through them, but beware of over exploitation.

# Preparing a short segment

It will be useful if you have the QCA schemes of work in your chosen language, especially Unit 10: Our sporting lives.

The QCA schemes of work for Key Stage 2 languages comprise 24 units, the first 12 of which are available as hard copy and 13–24 currently online. Each year has six units, so Units 1–6 are particularly suited to Year 3, Units 7–12 to Year 4, Units 13–18 to Year 5 and Units 19–24 to Year 6. Each unit is designed to take about five to six weeks, or roughly half a term. Units are themselves divided into shorter sections.

On the other hand, you may want to develop oracy skills further as you present and practise some new language items and Part 3:2, p19 indicates that as part of the repetition stage, additional steps include saying the language in different moods. In fact, you will find that when you move on from responding to simple rhymes and songs, to presenting and practising new vocabulary and structures related to a theme, exactly the same principles apply in terms of sequencing as in the little Year 3 examples.

For instance, let us imagine that you want children to be able to talk and write about what sports they do. You consult the learning objectives in the Key Stage 2 Framework and choose O4.2 *Use physical reponse to show recognition and understanding of specific words and phrases* and L4.1 *Read and understand a range of familiar written phrases*. You also consult the new QCA schemes of work for languages. We shall look at an example in French.

In Unit 10 of the QCA scheme of work you find the core language related to sport which the unit suggests on the back page:

> *Je joue au tennis/au cricket/au basket.*
> *Je fais du vélo/du skate/de la danse/de la natation.*

**PRACTICAL TASK** PRACTICAL TASK **PRACTICAL TASK** PRACTICAL TASK **PRACTICAL TASK**

(You need Unit 10 (and Unit 3) of the QCA schemes of work in the language of your choice.)
Consider the core language above.
- How are you going to present and practise this new language?
- What decisions do you have to make about teaching these expressions?

The QCA schemes of work, like the Framework, are non-statutory and intended to be used flexibly for your own situation. You do not have to follow them prescriptively. It is up to you to decide which items to present. When you look at the list, you may decide to select particularly the sports likely to be played by the children in your own class. So you reduce your list to tennis, cycling, skateboarding, dancing, swimming and basketball. However, you know that some children go to judo lessons, so you add in *le judo* or *je fais du judo.*

You then consider different ways of supporting children's understanding of what these expressions mean. You try out some different mimes. You consider collecting items of equipment or clothing for visual impact.

## Creating and using visuals

You find images in magazines and on the internet of some well-known sports personalities engaged in playing their sport. You also find some clipart which is easily available and make up a PowerPoint sequence. You print off some of the pictures to use as flash cards, and make smaller sets for table top activities. Your images might be similar to the ones below:

**Figure 4.1. Images that could be used to develop oracy skills**

**PRACTICAL TASK** PRACTICAL TASK PRACTICAL TASK PRACTICAL TASK PRACTICAL TASK

Consider the seven images above. What is the target language which each might depict? For example: *je nage – la natation – je fais de la natation*.

- Are the images equally suitable ?
- What do you need to bear in mind when choosing visuals to cue oral responses?

You might decide that some images like the tennis racquet and water bottle are rather static and seem to match *le tennis* rather than an expression with a verb. On the other hand, the boy on the skateboard seems to depict *je fais du skate*. You might choose the image of the children dancing because it a) is colourful, b) depicts children and c) shows the movement to go with *je fais de la danse*, or *je danse*.

**REFLECTIVE TASK**

Visuals from whatever source, need to be clear and unambiguous so that children recognise their meaning instantly. Which methods can you think of to check for clarity?

Be consistent in using visuals: flash cards, interactive whiteboard and PowerPoint images, small game playing cards for lotto, pelmanism or dominoes all need to be similar.

## Making the pattern clear

**PRACTICAL TASK** PRACTICAL TASK PRACTICAL TASK PRACTICAL TASK PRACTICAL TASK

Look again at the suggested core vocabulary and structures and the related images.

- What difficulties might some of these expressions pose for learners?
- How could you present the new language so as to make the patterns as clear as possible?
- Note these down for discussion.

(You would need to look to see what children had already learned and would probably revise or teach sports individually such as *le foot*. We shall consider prior learning in Chapter 5 on planning a whole lesson.)

You might decide to group the expressions in the following manner and colour code them appropriately, with the masculine expressions *au foot* and *du vélo* in blue, and the feminine *de la danse* in red.

Je nage

Je joue **au foot**
Je joue **au tennis**

Je fais **du skate**
Je fais **du judo**
Je fais **du vélo**

Je fais *de la danse*

## How many items?

Having clustered the vocabulary to make the patterns more transparent, you need to decide whether or not you are going to present all the items in a single lesson. Your decision will depend in part on the age and ability of your class, and how long they have already been learning the language. The younger the learners, the smaller the steps.

If your learners are in Year 4, say, you may begin just by introducing the first three: *je nage, je joue au foot* and *je joue au tennis*.

In a follow-up lesson you may introduce the three which go together with the new verb *faire: je fais + du skate, du judo* and *du vélo.* You present *du skate* and *du judo* before *du vélo*, because they are cognates and children will recognise them easily, as they do *au foot* and *au tennis*. In a third lesson you introduce the new pattern *je fais de la danse*.

Eventually you practise all the items together. On account of the variety of ways you conduct the presentation and practice phases, you do not need over long lists of vocabulary, although when there are several cognates, as there are with sports, you will be able to present more at a time than when there is little about the new vocabulary which is familiar. The presentation technique you use will depend on the nature of the vocabulary and will involve varied repetition strategies. Is it single word, phrases, questions and answers? Are you working at word, sentence or text level?

*Step 1: Exposure – just look and listen*

*Regardez-moi. Ecoutez. Ne répétez pas.*
Give children a chance to simply listen to the new vocabulary and/or structure without having to produce it themselves. They need time to absorb the new sounds before they reproduce them.

*Step 2: Listen and respond*

Model actions for different sports, or show images, saying the phrases and inviting children to copy the actions.

*Step 3: Listen and say, listen and repeat in a variety of ways*

*Ecoutez et répétez.*
Children next do the sports actions, repeating the words or phrases as you say them. When children have heard and responded in a number of ways, provide plenty of opportunities to repeat and practise the new language with as much variety as possible. Repetition work can become tedious for both children and their teacher if it is not delivered in a motivating way. As we saw in Chapter 2, teaching younger learners means you have an advantage over secondary languages teachers as regards responding and speaking. Young children are usually very keen to echo whatever you are saying and repeat with great enthusiasm.

This is where your use of body language (exaggerated gestures, intonation, facial expression) helps make the repetition phase memorable. Try repeating the new word(s) in different ways and varying the mood, for example loudly, quietly, fast, slowly, sadly, etc. Vary speed and volume – *plus vite, plus lentement, plus fort, plus bas*.

As well as using your own voice and body to cue these different kinds of repetition, you can create some simple visual cues to indicate *like a robot, like a ghost.* Figure 4.2 on page 42 shows some ideas.

---

**PRACTICAL TASK** PRACTICAL TASK PRACTICAL TASK PRACTICAL TASK PRACTICAL TASK

(You will need large felt markers and scrap card.)

In small groups create a simple visual to cue repetition in a particular manner.

- Try out your ideas with other trainees.
- Are your visuals clear and unambiguous enough?

---

Try **mouthing** the new words or phrases and inviting children to say aloud what they think you are saying. This encourages them to listen hard and watch the shape of your mouth. *Regardez ma bouche . . . .*

Another tactic to get children to say new words over and over again for you is to cup your hand behind your ear and with rising intonation say, *'Pardon? Pardon?'*

like a ghost

quickly

like a chorister

slowly

**Figure 4.2 Simple visual clues**

REFLECTIVE TASK

**REFLECTIVE TASK**

Remember:

- The vital **first time** a learner encounters the new language must be **memorable** in order for the new language to stick

- Learners need to **hear and repeat** the language **many times** if they are to internalise it and produce it independently.

- The art of repetition is to devise **many different ways** of letting children hear/say the same thing: good repetition activities should **make children want to participate.**

- Invite children to **repeat as a class** through teacher-led activities, then encourage **groups**, say, all the children round a table, or boys versus girls, and last of all, **individuals**.

### Developing a question and answer series

When children have repeated the new vocabulary in many fun ways, you need to help them remember the words and phrases by asking questions about the stimulus items.

At this point you need to sequence the questions you ask in a staged way. Do not immediately ask an open question along the lines of *Qu'est-ce que c'est?*

**Developing a question and answer sequence**

It is important to structure questions in ways which help all learners respond.

*Qu'est-ce que c'est?* is **not** always helpful as a **STARTER** question.

**Example 1: Using props (swimming goggles, mini football, tennis racket, helmet, judo belt, pictures, flash cards) or mimes**

**Here is a simple version based on the names of the sports.**
Introduce each item with **repetition techniques.** Remember: *Regardez-moi. Ecoutez. Ne répétez pas.*
*Voici le judo. Voici le tennis. Voici le foot.*
*Maintenant répétez.* **Practise with varying repetition techniques.**

If necessary, insert an **intermediate stage** by placing a letter/number next to each prompt and asking *Le judo. C'est quelle lettre? C.*

**Then move on to graded questions.**
Start with yes/no – *oui/non.* True false recognition – *vrai/faux.*

| | | |
|---|---|---|
| *C'est le tennis?* (rising intonation) | *Oui.* | Positive prompts |
| *C'est le foot?* (rising intonation) | *Oui.* | (*C'est le foot*) |
| *C'est le judo?* | *Non.* | Negative prompts |
| *C'est le football? Oui ou non?* | *Non.* | |

**Follow with alternatives:**

| | |
|---|---|
| A: *C'est le foot ou le tennis?* | *Le tennis.* |
| B: *C'est le tennis ou le judo?* | *Le tennis.* |
| C: *C'est le tennis, le judo ou le foot?* | *Le foot.* |
| D: *C'est le skate, le tennis, le judo ou le foot?* | *Le skate.* |

**A is easier for children than B, and C is easier than D.**

Questioning stage – finish with open questions – no support in the question for the answer:

| | |
|---|---|
| *Qu'est-ce que c'est?* | *Le skate.* |

**Example 2:** *Using verb constructions*
Stimulus question: *Qu'est-ce que tu fais?*
Show visuals: *Je nage. Je joue au tennis. Je joue au foot.*

| | |
|---|---|
| Visual: *Je nage – oui ou non? (Vrai ou faux?)* | *Oui.* (Visual matches statement.) |
| Visual: *Je joue au foot – oui ou non?* | *Non.* (Visual does not match statement.) |

**Then give some options.**

Show visual of *je joue au tennis.*
Ask: *Je joue au foot OU je joue au tennis?* (two correctly phrased alternatives)

Last statement matches the visual you are showing.
Pupil says in response to the alternatives: *au tennis* or *je joue au tennis*.

A slightly more challenging option. You show a visual of *je joue an tennis* as before but you give the two alternatives in a different order. This time the answer you want is given first and the first statement matches the visual.
So you say: *Je joue au tennis OU je je joue au foot.*
The pupil replies: *au tennis* or *je joue au tennis*.
This is harder than the first example because children have to hold in their head the prompt *je joue au tennis* while listening to *je joue au foot*.

**The question contains the correct structure.**

Intermediate stage: Put a number you have already taught children against the different visuals either on the whiteboard or on the cards themselves.
*Je fais de la danse. C'est **quel numéro?***          **15**

More challenging still:
Visual of judo: *Je fais **du judo**, je fais du skate ou*      ***du judo/je fais du judo***
*je fais de la danse?*                               *(several choices)*

Finally: **Open question**

Qu-est-ce que tu fais?                      Je fais de la danse.

No support is given and this is not a communicative quesion where children are asked a genuine question. Here the children can all see the visual you are showing and the questions are simply display questions – i.e. you are asking the children in order to get them to practise the vocabulary and the structure but everybody can see it is tennis or football or whatever. This is a PFL or practice foreign language sequence, not a CFL or communicative foreign language sequence.

Open questions can form part of games.
**Remove a card.** Please say **which one is missing.**
*Voici le skate, le vélo, la danse, le judo, le tennis. Fermez les yeux.*
Take away skateboarding
*Ouvrez les yeux. Qu'est-ce qui manque?*           Le skate.

# Practising new language

Here are ideas for practising new language. You can find numerous examples throughout the Framework and in the QCA schemes of work and support materials.

- Imagine children are struggling to remember *emploi du temps*. Invite them to build up the expression a word at a time starting with *emploi*. They continue *emploi du*, then *emploi du temps*. Front chaining is building up *emploi, emploi du, emploi du temps*.
- You can also practise building up a longer word or expression backwards so children say *temps*, then *du temps*, then *emploi du temps*. This is called back chaining.

- **Ping-pong**: You can 'bat' the first word or syllable to the class, who bat the second word or syllable back to you – you say *emploi* and make a batting gesture with your hand or a real table tennis bat, and they say *du* and bat it back to you, then you return *temps*. if you were batting syllables you could bat *em*, they could return *ploi*, you bat *du*, they bat *temps*, etc. This is particularly good for long compound German words. Children can practise ping-pong with vocabulary and verb parts in pairs or the teacher can play against the whole class.
- Children repeat a word X times, quickly.
- Children repeat cues within a given time *contre la montre*.
- As a chain – children repeat a series adding a new item each time.
- Sing the words to a simple well known tune.
- Repeat if it's true: *répétez si c'est vrai…*
- Label visuals with a number/letter – *C'est quel numéro, je fais de la danse?*

## Using a small amount of language in many different ways

With young language learners a real skill is recycling language frequently but at the same time keeping children motivated by presenting and practising new language over and over again in lots of game-like formats. Listening and speaking activities need to be followed, when appropriate for your learners, with reading and writing tasks. To explore this further, try the following.

**PRACTICAL TASK** PRACTICAL TASK PRACTICAL TASK PRACTICAL TASK PRACTICAL TASK

(You need your Key Stage 2 Framework Part 3:2 p21 and Part 3.2 pages 23–30.)

In this section you will find four 15-minute sessions, which reinforce learning throughout the week. These short sessions are linked to the medium- and longer-term plans also in Part 3. Read the outlines for the four short sessions and then continue with Part 3, p23–30.

- As the Framework is non-language specific, try planning the language of your choice into some of these examples.
- Use these ideas to support you in your own preparation and teaching.

## Trying out repetition and question and answer techniques

**PRACTICAL TASK** PRACTICAL TASK PRACTICAL TASK PRACTICAL TASK PRACTICAL TASK

(You will need the QCA schemes of work and the teacher trainee support materials.)

Working individually, choose a topic area in your selected language from one of the units in the QCA schemes of work. It would provide more variety if different people in your group chose different units.

- From your chosen unit, select one section, and from this section prepare one element for a 10–15 minute slot.
- Choose your visuals or props carefully and plan how you would present and practise the new language items, using varied repetition and question and answer techniques.
- Deliver your segment to a small group of your peers, using your chosen resources.

# Primary Languages in action – developing speaking skills using the Key Stage 2 Framework

It is important to extend children beyond repetition and question and answer sequences of the presentation and practice type. Let us now look at how spoken interaction is encouraged within the Key Stage 2 Framework for Languages through the provision of lots of opportunities to interact with you and with each other, answering questions and, most importantly, learning to ask questions too (see Oracy 3.3).

## REFLECTIVE TASK

Incorporate lots of short bursts of pair work in your lessons. Why do you think that this will be helpful to children?

## PRACTICAL TASK PRACTICAL TASK PRACTICAL TASK PRACTICAL TASK PRACTICAL TASK

(You will need access to the Primary Languages Training Zone.)

Go the Oracy section and choose the **German conversation model**. In this extract, the children are practising the skills of **listening and speaking**. Notice how the teacher models each of the responses, before asking children the question. Watch the extract a couple of times.

● How do you think the use of the soft toy helps children?

● Have you observed any teachers in your placement schools using props in a similar way to stimulate a conversation?

Explore ways of making your classroom a secure environment in which children are encouraged to have a go and take risks with the new language. Promote appropriate accuracy, especially of pronunciation, but deal with mistakes sensitively.

## Encouraging children to speak: puppets and soft toys

As we can see from the video example, young children are usually less inhibited when speaking to or through a puppet, either to each other or to the teacher. It is easy to make envelope or paper bag or even (clean) sock puppets, so that each child has a puppet and conversations can take place between the puppets, rather than the children. Try giving the puppets or soft toys a name in the new language and perhaps a particular kind of character – shy, grumpy, sleepy. Using props like this lowers what Krashen (1984) calls the *affective filter*, the barrier of awkwardness which sometimes overcomes language learners when they have to speak in the new language.

# Literacy in the Key Stage 2 Framework for Languages

The Key Stage 2 Framework makes clear that literacy skills should be developed alongside children's aural–oral skills and that they mutually reinforce each other.

*The literacy skills of reading and writing are supported by, and in turn, reinforce the development of oracy. They are likely to take on greater prominence as children become familiar with the relationship between sounds and writing and letters/characters in the new language and apply this knowledge in reading and writing.*

(DfES, 2005, p8)

---

**PRACTICAL TASK** PRACTICAL TASK PRACTICAL TASK PRACTICAL TASK PRACTICAL TASK

(You will need your Key Stage 2 Framework.)

Read through the Literacy objectives on page 19 *At a Glance* for Year 3, concentrating just on the objectives relating to reading.

- How well does what is described match up with the experiences of reading you have encountered in schools?

---

**Literacy 3.2 makes links between some phonemes, rhymes and spellings, and read aloud familiar words.** How might we help children to do this?

When we considered oracy in the first part of this chapter, we saw that children can be encouraged to listen out for specific words within rhymes and songs. Of course this also applies to phonemes. One way is to take a phonic sound for consideration each week. If your rhyme or song contains several phonemes, everybody can listen for all the sounds, or alternatively, you can allocate a different sound with a different gesture to different groups in the class to listen out for. Invite children to identify sounds which are the same as or different from English. There is a spotlight on using traditional songs to train the ear in Part 2:3, p36.

Alternatively listen out for pairs of rhyming words. You can see and hear an example of this on the Primary Languages Training Zone.

---

**PRACTICAL TASK** PRACTICAL TASK PRACTICAL TASK PRACTICAL TASK PRACTICAL TASK

(You will need access to www.primarylanguages.org.uk.)

Go to Oracy and choose Keyhole numbers. You will see a teacher using a little poem in German *eins, zwei, Polizei* to emphasise some rhyming words. *Eins, zwei, die reimen sich.* How would you draw children's attention to the graphemes which match the phonemes? What are children likely to find tricky about how the numbers are written? Find other rhymes in your language which could be exploited in a similar way. Share examples.

---

A common sound in French is *oi*. Invite children to brainstorm words they think have the *oi* sound in. They might come up with *au revoir, trois, noir, poisson*. Write the words up on the board or interactive whiteboard and highlight the sound–spelling link.

# Listen and read

Many primary schools use phonic clouds as mobiles. Each cloud focuses on one particular sound, which may be represented by a number of different graphemes. Each time a new word which includes one of the phonemes is met, add an extra cloud to the mobile. Or you can simply cluster sounds on word cards on a display board, adding new ones to the different categories as they occur.

You can adapt several games which you might normally play with visuals or pictures as prompts, by using graphemes instead.

### Play phoneme–grapheme lotto

In this version of lotto, the squares contain the graphemes for various phonemes, i.e. *on*, *oi*, Two versions can be played. First, read out the various phonemes and the children select the appropriate grapheme on their paper. Next, read out words containing one of the phonemes, which children must hear in their heads within the whole word and then choose the appropriate grapheme.

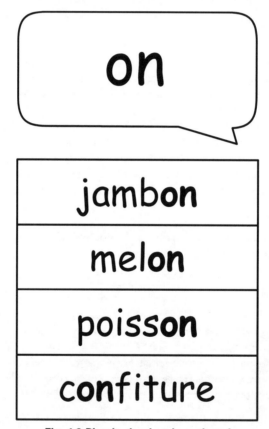

**Fig. 4.3 Phonic cloud and word cards**

### Phoneme–grapheme stations

Stick phonic cards around the school hall, or even in different parts of your classroom. You then say a series of words containing the different phonemes. Children run to the 'correct' card, or, if you have limited space, point to the one with the grapheme they think matches the phoneme. You start with just two phonemes and very gradually incorporate more. Make this more challenging by eventually including words such as *poisson*, which include more than one phoneme. In this case children then have to choose which of two cards to run to, either the one with *on* or the one with *oi*. Ask someone to explain to you after they have arrived why they chose the card they did.

## Noughts and crosses
Another possibility is to play noughts and crosses *(morpion)* with graphemes in the boxes, or alternatively words containing the chosen graphemes. You can see an example of this on the Primary Languages Training Zone.

---

**PRACTICAL TASK** PRACTICAL TASK PRACTICAL TASK PRACTICAL TASK PRACTICAL TASK

**Literacy – speaking and reading – sound game**

Go to the Key Stage 2 Framework. Select Literacy then Sound game. Here you can see an HLTA who has been working on a World War 2 cross-curricular project using words from the story text to play noughts and crosses to practise the French sounds *en* and *an* as in *danger*.

- Watch the extract and write down how the teacher is using particular words from the cross-curricular project story text to demonstrate GPCs.
- Discuss in your group other sounds which it would be useful to highlight and how you might find a context in which to practise them.
- How might you adapt this activity or the phoneme–grapheme lotto above to use with a class with whom you are familiar?

---

### Literacy 3.1 to recognise some familiar words in written form
Note here the inclusion of the word 'familiar'. This means that you will be encouraging children to match familiar words to pictures, symbols or objects – but the words have already been met orally first.

# Read and respond

In just the same way as children first responded with actions when listening, encourage them to respond by doing something in response to a **familiar written text**. Make word or phrase cards of classroom instructions, which they are very used to hearing you say, such as *écoutez* or *levez-vous.* Children **read** the instructions and do a mime or the appropriate action.

Invite children to match written captions or words to picture flash cards, for example the names of pets – all of which they know how to pronounce well. Of course, you can do this on the interactive whiteboard too, using the drag and drop facility.

When children are really good at linking particular phoneme combinations with their graphemes, challenge them to predict how new words which they have not yet met might be pronounced. If you are teaching French, a wall display of numbers 1–12 in words can support them making the sound–spelling links. This can be linked to dictionary work.

| **un** d**eu**x tr**oi**s quatre c**in**q six |
|---|
| sept huit n**eu**f d**i**x **on**ze d**ou**ze |

# Read and repeat

For example, when presenting the sports items we considered above, having practised saying the sports, you need to show word flashcards and encourage children to read and repeat. Discuss what the class notice about the pronunciation of *sport* and *sports* in French. As you read aloud, can they hear that the final *t* and final *s* are silent? Are there any other words in French that they have learned, which also have unpronounced final letters?

### Primary Languages in action

For the next task you will need to access the Training Zone at www.primarylanguages.org. uk. This will give you an opportunity to see this literacy objective being demonstrated.

---

**PRACTICAL TASK** PRACTICAL TASK PRACTICAL TASK PRACTICAL TASK PRACTICAL TASK

**Literacy – planets flashcard reading game with interactive whiteboard**

In this video extract the teacher is running a game which involves the children reading the names of planets on word flashcards and then, two at a time working in teams, trying to be the first to touch the matching picture on the interactive whiteboard.

- Watch the clip several times.
- How does the teacher involve all the class in the reading activity and not just the two children at the board?

---

# Moving from word through sentence to text level

### Literacy 4.1 to read and understand a range of familiar written phrases:

Once again, children are working with familiar language, although they are extending their reading from individual words to phrases and simple sentences.

### Literacy 5.1 to re-read frequently a variety of short texts:

We can see here the development from sentence to text level. For example, children could recreate the text from a rhyme, story or song by reassembling sentence strips to make the correct order.

---

**REFLECTIVE TASK**

Look for some story books suitable for reading for meaning in the new language at your chosen key stage. (This will be an appropriate task for when you are abroad too.)

As well as those originally intended for native speaker children, look for versions of well known stories from English in the new language, for example *The Hungry Caterpillar* or *We're Going on a Bear Hunt*.

- Share with each other the books you have found and discuss what makes them good stories to use for developing literacy skills alongside reading for pleasure.
- List together the features of a good book for storytelling and reading together.

---

If you cannot find a suitable foreign language version of stories to share, place sticky notes with the new text on top of the English words. This works particularly well with Big Books, many of which you will be familiar with from the curriculum in English. Some publishers are willing for you to make an electronic version of their story books provided you have specific permission and have purchased your own copy of the book. (Please check this thoroughly as not all publishers permit this.) However, if the pictures and text are scanned in and shown using a data projector, the whole class can see illustrations in some excellent story books, which are sometimes rather too small for class use.

# Developing writing skills using the Key Stage 2 Framework

In many Primary Languages programmes in the recent past, literacy skills, and writing in particular, have been intentionally omitted or have appeared in a very limited fashion. So why is writing important for Primary Languages?

Writing:
- reinforces the association between the sound and the word;
- gives the language a relevance and meaning;
- creates the possibility of real communication exchanges with children in the new language.

**Literacy 3.3** suggests that children should *experiment with the writing of simple words.* Note again the inclusion of the word *familiar* in the bullet point beneath the heading, reminding us to build on what children already know well through listening, speaking and reading.

Children need to hear, speak and see the words many times before they write them. When children are confident with sound spelling links they will be able to use this knowledge to experiment with writing short words and phrases.

What kinds of activities could children do in order to meet this objective? Spotlights on Emergent writing in the play corner (L3.1) in Part 2:3, p38 gives an example.

There are many ways in which children can practise writing in the new language. They can trace words in the air, or on a partner's back or hand, (sometimes this is more effective if the recipients shut their eyes while the tracing is being done, as it helps them concentrate on the shapes being made). Children can write on their mini whiteboards, on paper, on the inter-active whiteboard and in the sand tray. The Framework also states that children should write *using a model* and later, write *some single words from memory*.

**PRACTICAL TASK** PRACTICAL TASK PRACTICAL TASK PRACTICAL TASK PRACTICAL TASK

(You will need to look at the Training Zone.)

For an alternative approach, open Using the Key Stage 2 Framework and click on Literacy. Within the Literacy examples, select Gap filling.

In this extract the children are writing words in the gaps using the models on word cards. They then read their completed sentences aloud.

- How has the teacher prepared the children to carry out the activity with confidence and ease?

## Copy writing

At the time of writing, evidence about Primary Language learners' writing skills in England is still being gathered. However, we do know from research that some Year 7 beginner learners of French found copywriting particularly difficult to tackle. This appeared to be due, at least in part, to GPC mismatches. Although the Year 7 learners were attempting to 'sound out' the words they were trying to copy, without a thorough knowledge of GPCs (which they had not been taught), the process was not very successful, as they were trying to hold spellings which had no particular patterns for them in their minds as they were copywriting.

This indicates strongly, as we stated earlier, that we should explicitly teach children how to recognise and apply GPC from the start of foreign language learning in the primary phase, so that sounding out is more accurate and learners can confidently predict what spellings might be, using their knowledge of sound–spelling links. Children need to be told the purpose of copy writing. The Key Stage 2 Framework says:

> *From an early age children become familiar with the relationship between sounds and letters/characters and* apply these in their reading and spelling.
>
> (DfES 2005: 2:4 p52 [my emphasis])

Writing should serve the purpose of:

- supporting the other skills;
- fixing what has been learned;
- being used as a model for future reference;
- acting as a record of work covered.

Boh the Key Stage 2 Framework and the supporting documentation from QCA supply us with a multitude of ideas for literacy-related activities, so we shall not enumerate them again here. However, two final points need to be made.

Firstly, language learners need to write with a purpose and for a real audience where possible.

For example, children can communicate real messages by writing and sending emails – these may simply be to another class in your school, but could be to a Year 7 class in an associated secondary school or to a partner class in a school abroad.

If you consult page 15 of the Teacher's guide for the new QCA schemes of work for languages, you will find examples of literacy-related activities. How many of them have you tried out so far?

# Free writing

Secondly, encourage children to begin to create their own pieces of writing. Use supports such as writing frames and provide regular access to dictionaries and word lists to enable them to express their own meanings and begin to go beyond the formulaic chunks.

Below is part of a little poem about Easter that children can adapt.

> *C'était Pâques le matin*
> *J'ai trouvé dans mon jardin*
> *Des œufs jaunes comme le soleil*

*Des œufs <u>rouges</u> comme <u>les tulipes</u>*
*Des œufs <u>verts</u> comme <u>les prés</u>*

Here is how one Year 5 child adapted it by changing the underlined adjectives and nouns.

*C'était Pâques le matin*
*J'ai trouvé dans mon jardin*
*Des œufs <u>gris</u> comme <u>les lapins</u>*
*Des œufs <u>rouges</u> comme <u>les vins</u>*
*Des œufs <u>dorés</u> comme <u>les pains</u>*
*Des œufs <u>oranges</u> comme <u>les poissons</u>*
*Des œufs <u>marron</u> comme <u>les violons</u>*
*Des œufs <u>roses</u> comme <u>les cochons</u>*

In Year 6 some children will be able to adapt a short story such as *The Old Woman who Swallowed a Fly* to create their own tale.

# Daily practice opportunities

Do not forget that in addition to discrete language lessons, you will need to consolidate language learning by means of five-minute slots, such as joining in a rhyme together, singing a song, or carrying out daily routines using the new language. This incidental use of language should also be planned. There are also spotlights on using everyday routines including the register in Part 2:3, pages 31 and 32 and in Part 3:3, p34.

---

A SUMMARY OF **KEY POINTS**

> Skills should be taught in combination. Listening and speaking are often linked, as are listening and reading, reading and writing.

> As part of the Oracy strand of the Key Stage 2 Framework it is vital to give children lots of opportunities to listen and respond via listen and do activities before asking them to respond verbally.

> Explore ways of helping children develop accurate pronunciation habits.

> Time spent teaching GPCs is time well spent.

> As a general rule, learners need to hear, speak and see the words before they write them.

> Teach literacy skills from the outset but make explicit connections between the spoken and written word.

> Make the purpose of any copywriting clear.

> Explore ways of supporting children to engage in free writing.

---

**MOVING** *ON* > > > **>** **>** **>** MOVING *ON* > > > **>** **>** **>** MOVING *ON*

Both the Key Stage 2 Framework and the QCA schemes of work and support materials incorporate many practical suggestions for teaching and learning activities for developing oracy and literacy. Simply reading the Spotlights throughout the Framework will be an excellent way of helping you see how the objectives can be translated into practice. They are highlighted in grey-blue boxes so that you can spot them. Take time to really explore these and try to build up an increasing repertoire for yourself.

**FURTHER READING** FURTHER READING **FURTHER READING** FURTHER READING

CILT/TDA (2008) *Teacher trainee support material for QCA's A scheme of work for Key Stage 2*. London: CILT.

Comfort, T. and Tierney, D. (2007) *We have the technology*. Young Pathfinder 14. London: CILT.

Molzan, J. and Lloyd, S. (2001) *Le manuel phonique*. Essex: Jolly Learning Ltd.

QCA (2007) *French/German/Spanish. A scheme of work for Key Stage 2*. London: Qualifications and Curriculum Authority. Each language available separately with a very useful *Teacher's guide: Languages – a scheme of work for Key Stage 2*.

Skarbek, C. (1997) *First steps to reading and writing*. Young Pathfinder 5. London: CILT.

All the Young Pathfinder series for primary teachers are full of practical teaching suggestions.

## Useful websites

www.standards.dcsf.gov.uk/schemes for QCA schemes of work.

# 5
# Putting the Key Stage 2 Framework into practice: starting to plan

By the end of this chapter you will have:

- considered short-term planning in more detail;
- linked planning to the Key Stage 2 Framework and QCA schemes of work;
- become aware of the components of effective lessons plans;
- reflected on the use of a template to structure your planning;
- recognised the need to plan according to clear learning objectives;
- appreciated the need to build Assessment for Learning (AfL) into your planning.

This chapter addresses the following Professional Standards for QTS:
Q2, Q5, Q7a, Q10, Q14, Q15, Q22

## Planning: getting started

Thorough and systematic planning is fundamental to effective teaching. In the course of your initial teacher training, you will have encountered some of the basic practical principles of planning that are generic across all curriculum areas, such as:

- having a clear learning intention or learning objective;
- revisiting prior knowledge;
- providing opportunities to apply existing skills in new contexts.

Planning provides you with a clear idea of what you wish the children to have achieved in a given time frame. It is about making the links between prior and new learning explicit. To ensure this, you need to scaffold the process through carefully planned activities. As with other subjects, considerations for long- and medium-term planning will be different from those for short-term planning at the level of individual lessons or weekly plans.

Having briefly considered the presentation and practice phases of a short lesson segment in Chapter 4, we continue with planning a whole Primary Languages lesson. Of course, when you are in school, your lesson plans will need to be part of a **unit of work**, which in turn is part of a **scheme of work**, and particularly if you are the Primary Languages Co-ordinator, you will want to consider the long-term plans into which the other plans fit.

## Short-term planning/planning individual lessons

REFLECTIVE TASK

In pairs consider the Primary Languages template on the adjacent pages.

**Table 5.1. Template for Primary Languages lesson plan**

| Primary Languages Lesson Plan | Date & start/ end time | Class/Yr | No of pupils | IEPs | AT (KS2) 1 L  2 S  3 R  4 W Level | Topic: QCA SoW ref |
|---|---|---|---|---|---|---|
| **Resources:** (including other adults) | | | | **Cross-curricular links** (e.g. ICT, literacy, numeracy, PSHCE) | | **KS2 Framework links**<br><br>Oracy<br><br>Literacy<br><br>Intercultural Understanding |
| **Self evaluation: Did children meet the LOs?**<br><br>How do I know?<br><br>Who did not meet them?<br><br>Who exceeded them?<br><br>Action for these children | | | | **Core learning objectives (vocab., grammar, pronunciation):** by the end of the lesson, most learners will be able to:<br><br>**Differentiated objectives:**<br>• **Less able** learners may<br><br>• **More able** learners may<br><br>**Language Learning Strategies** | | |
| **New vocab/grammar/KAL:** | | | | **Essential prior learning:** What do they know already? Will I need to revise anything? | | |

| Time | Activity with (A)ssessment opportunities and (D)ifferentiation | Target language What I am going to say |
|---|---|---|
| | **Starter** | |
| | Shared objectives | |
| | **Main**<br>Presentation | |
| | Practice | |
| | Production | |
| | **Plenary** | |
| | **Next lesson/follow up** | |

- Draw up together a list of the key features of the plan which you notice.
- Why do we need these headings to help us plan in detail?
- Which parts of the plan are particularly useful?

Share your findings as a whole group with your tutor.

Individual schools and Higher Education Institutions will have their specific planning templates. However, we suggest that you ensure that your plans incorporate the following headings as a checklist:

- reference to and revisiting of **prior learning**;
- **lesson objective** specific to the session or sessions;
- **teaching and learning activities** representing specific phases of the lesson with approximate **timings** – these may reference knowledge about language and language learning strategies as appropriate;
- opportunities for **differentiation** and **assessment**;
- **plenary** including **evaluation** and **next steps**;
- **space for a brief self-evaluation of your own teaching**.

A Primary Languages lesson needs to include in addition an indication of the **target language**: what you plan to say at specific points in the lesson, especially for instructions.

You will notice that the template includes a first page of administrative and organisational details: class, time of day, individual needs, topic, references to non-statutory frameworks (in our case the Key Stage 2 Framework for Languages) and schemes of work (the QCA schemes of work for Key Stage 2 Languages).

You will find the new teacher trainee support materials accompanying the QCA schemes of work especially helpful in showing specific and explicit cross-curricular links in the box headed *National Curriculum Links.*

## REFLECTIVE TASK

Links to other curriculum areas are an important means of revisiting concepts in different contexts. List some examples.

You need to decide where your lesson fits into the medium-term plan or the unit of work. A unit of work usually covers about half a term, so a period of five to six weeks. If we assume that schools are offering an hour a week for Primary Languages in accordance with Framework recommendations, then a unit of work is five to six lessons, each of one hour. Of course, you will probably deliver the hour entitlement as several shorter slots of perhaps twenty or thirty minutes each. Whatever the length of the session, each lesson should build on the one before it, in a sequence of lessons which eventually form a unit of work. So before you begin to flesh out your plan, you need to ask yourself:

- What is my lesson **building on**?
- What have children learned **already**?
- What do they **already know**?
- What do they **already understand**?
- What can they **already do**?

This helps to ensure that you are building on previous learning and your lesson is not in a vacuum. This is why the QCA schemes of work have clear sections on the first page of each unit entitled *About this unit*, *Where the unit fits in* and *Prior learning*.

If we take a specific example, say of Unit 10 *Our sporting lives*, which we focused on in Chapter 4, you will see that some of the new French language content is the names of sports used in conjunction with the verbs *jouer* and *faire*. You will see that Unit 3 has already introduced some words for sports in expressions using verbs and *bien*, i.e. *je nage bien* (rather than *la natation*). Children have also met one example with *jouer au* in *je joue bien au foot*.

Next ask yourself:

- What do I want children to **learn now**?
- What precisely do I want them to be **able to do**?

At this point you must be precise about the **vocabulary** and **structures** that you want the children to learn. Be specific!

What **exactly** do I want children to:

- **know**;
- **understand**;
- be able to **say**;
- be able to **read**;
- be able to **write**;

by the end of the lesson?

When you plan a lesson which is part of a series on a particular theme, keep in mind how you want children to be able to use the new language at the end of the topic. Looking at the medium-term plan or unit as a whole helps you with these decisions about the smaller steps you want children to take towards your end of unit goal. It may mean several lessons working towards the same outcome. On the final page of each QCA unit of work you will see an *End of unit activity*. Because it is helpful to also bear this end point in mind right at the beginning of the planning process, the trainee support materials have moved this end of unit activity **forward** to the first overview page for each unit.

## REFLECTIVE TASK

Deciding in advance what you want as an outcome – not only in terms of product but in terms of quality or quantity – helps you design your individual lessons. Can you think of some examples?

# Expressing learning objectives clearly

Deciding on a clear learning objective is key to effective lesson planning. Be very specific about what you want children to achieve. Think about what you want learners to be able to 'do' at the end of your Primary Languages lesson which they could not do when they started. Learning objectives must describe the learning outcomes, not a list of activities. A learning objective must be **achievable** and should be able to be **measured**, in other words, you (and the learners) should be able to tell whether the learners have met your objective or not. This is important for you at the self-evaluation stage when you are reviewing your lesson, having delivered it.

Remember, the expression 'use' the language, can refer to any one or combination of the skills of understanding, listening, speaking, reading, writing, as well as to knowledge and understanding related to intercultural understanding. Children may also be developing knowledge about language and language learning strategies.

## REFLECTIVE TASK
REFLECTIVE TASK

Here are some examples of learning objectives. Working in groups, consider these and note down why you think they are effective or why you think they do not meet the criteria above.

- Say numbers 1–10 sequentially.
- Know the names of animals.
- Talk about sports.
- Learn numbers 10–20.
- Join in with [song] with an action.
- Read a story.
- Make a Christmas card.
- Be able to pronounce [the following words] accurately.

**Understanding** the new language is very different from being able to **speak, read or write** it. A learning objective expressed in a general way such as *To know the names of animals* is not very helpful, as it is too vague. Which kinds of animals are we talking about? Are they pets, farm or zoo animals? How many are we aiming to teach? Which ones are they? Do we want learners to know the genders? Are we going to expect them to spell them correctly or only pronounce them? A more precise learning objective is *Be able to pronounce accurately six animal names*. This clear focus helps both teachers and learners to identify success criteria and makes assessment easier.

## PRACTICAL TASK PRACTICAL TASK PRACTICAL TASK PRACTICAL TASK PRACTICAL TASK

(You need your QCA schemes of work for Key Stage 2 and the grid on page 61.)

Allocate to each of you, one of the units from the new QCA schemes of work for Key Stage 2 in the language of your choice, so that different people are working on different units.

- Using a marker pen, highlight the key words and phrases used to describe learning objectives (expectations) relating them to the skills of listening, speaking, reading and writing. (For this task, consider what **most** learners will be able to do and use columns 1–4 only.)
- Note useful expressions in the appropriate columns in the grid on page 61.
- Share your findings with each other and compile a fuller list during the debrief. An example is done for you.

## Approaches to planning

### Formulating lesson objectives more precisely

**Using the QCA Sceme of work for Key Stage 2, note down under the appropriate columns for the different skills, key language which helps express objectives clearly.**

**At the end of the lesson, *most* learners will be able to:**

| AT1 Listening | AR2 Speaking | AT3 Reading | AT4 Writing | Some (less able) | Others (more able) |
|---|---|---|---|---|---|
| Understand language spoken by the teacher | Request help in the TL  Identify | Understand written descriptions | Copy (accurately) | With prompting | From memory |
| | | | | | |

The following are examples of phrases you might like to consider using when writing learning objectives for short-term plans. At the end of the lesson children will be able to:

- understand X when they hear;
- understand X when they see;
- pronounce X accurately/clearly;
- recognise X <vocabulary>;
- listen and respond [including physical responses];
- recall <vocabulary>;
- use <vocabulary> in context;
- respond to <question> (consider physical responses);
- read and understand;
- read aloud with accurate pronunciation;
- write from a model;
- write [sentences] about [topic] using a writing frame/list of words and phrases;
- write from memory <vocabulary>;
- spell X correctly, including appropriate gender and accents.

Try to think in terms of not **how many words** children know but how **they are able to use them**. For example, as Deevoy states, knowing five animal names and being able to use them to answer questions such as:

- What colour is...
- What is...called?
- How many...are there?
- Which is the smallest/largest?
- Which is your favourite?

is more useful than knowing 20 names but only being able to recite them as a list of nouns parrot fashion from flashcards.

Be realistic about **how much new language** you feel your class can confidently tackle in a lesson. Depending on the age, abilities and needs of your particular class, plan bite-size pieces of new language, two or three new words as part of a topic, or a new phrase or structure, perhaps as part of a question and answer. Think **quality not quantity**. It is preferable to do a little really well than a lot badly.

### REFLECTIVE TASK

Avoid having too many learning objectives by keeping your focus very clear in planning.

## Differentiation

Having decided on the main learning objective(s) for your Primary Languages lesson, you need to think about differentiating them. Ask yourself:

- Do I want all the children to be able to do the same thing?
- Will I need to differentiate?

Consider what is manageable for the majority of children in your class. Then think of what some (the lower achievers perhaps) should be able to do – this may mean fewer words, but it could mean with more support. So for instance, *Our sporting lives* suggests *some children will respond with an action to prompts about sporting activities*. Finally, consider how others (the higher achievers) could be extended. This could be remembering more, or knowing the genders as well as the words, or being able to do something from memory or with more confidence. *Our Sporting lives* suggests that, in addition, some children may be able to express an opinion about the sports or could look for new vocabulary in a bilingual dictionary and apply it accurately when writing.

**PRACTICAL TASK** PRACTICAL TASK PRACTICAL TASK PRACTICAL TASK PRACTICAL TASK

**Expressing differentiated objectives**

(You need your Key Stage 2 scheme of work and the grid on page 61.)

Looking at another unit from the QCA schemes of work.

- Work with a different partner to list any expressions you find which are helpful in order to express differentiated objectives. This time use columns 5 and 6 to describe what some/other children may be able to do.
- Complete the table on page 61 and then pool your findings. An example is done for you.

You can find guidance on inclusion, including addressing the particular needs of children with special educational needs, gifted and talented children and learners for whom English is a second or additional language, in the Key Stage 2 Framework Part 2:1, p11 and in Part 3:4 p47–63.

In addition, each of the sections within the units in the QCA schemes of work and the new trainee support materials indicate opportunities for offering support and extension; in the former they are listed at the end of each section, in the latter they are in a column adjacent to the Framework objectives.

Differentiation can be offered by:

- task (providing different tasks for different learners);
- support (providing more or less scaffolding for different learners);
- outcome (expecting different outcomes from the task for different learners).

Some of your secondary languages colleagues may be able to support you in adapting your activities and worksheets as this is an area where they often have considerable expertise.

# Sharing objectives with children

It is now standard practice to share learning objectives with children, either verbally and/or by having them on display. You can write them on the board, interactive whiteboard or a poster, and read them together with the children. If the learning objectives are on view throughout the lesson, you can tick them off during the session as you address them, which gives children a sense of achievement and helps you keep the lesson focused.

Having the learning objectives visible and referring to them in the course of the lesson and again at the end (see plenary), supports:

- assessment, as children can reflect to see if they feel they have achieved them;
- your self-evaluation (did I achieve my objectives?).

You can make your learning objectives explicit by statements such as:

- By the end of the lesson, we will have learned how/about/to...
- We are learning to...
- By the end of the lesson **most of you** will be able to...
- **Some** of you will be able to...
- **Others** of you will have gone a bit further and will be able to...

Children need to understand the difference between what you want them **to do** (activities) and what you want them **to learn**.

Sharing learning objectives will be more effective, if you create success criteria, either beforehand, or in discussion with the children. For example, you can say to children:

- How will we know if we have achieved this?
- What you need to do to achieve this is...'
- Remember to...

## REFLECTIVE TASK

Framing success criteria helps children develop self-assessment skills and are useful during the plenary.

Sharing learning objectives helps children to see the point of what you are teaching and they are learning.

### Child speak: expressing learning objectives in a way that children can understand

The language you use to describe your learning objectives should be appropriate for the children in your class. It is often helpful if you think of your objectives in the way in which children will talk about them in the plenary. Examples might be:

- I can name six sports in French.
- I can say which sports I like.
- I can say which sports I do not like.
- I can say on which day of the week I play a sport.
- I can make a long sentence by joining two sentences about sports together with the connective *mais*.
- I can take part in a short conversation about sports with a talk partner.

Having formulated your learning objectives, you need to structure your Primary Languages lesson in a similar way to how you would other foundation subjects. This means structuring it as a series of episodes by separating the learning into distinct stages or steps, each of which has a specific outcome.

# Structuring the lesson

## Starter

Each lesson should begin with something familiar and follow a similar pattern. This provides a clear starting point and helps learners feel secure, as they know what to expect and what is expected of them. This is particularly important in the Foundation Stage and Key Stage 1, but benefits less confident learners in Key Stage 2 as well.

A familiar start might simply consist of an exchange of greetings: *Levez-vous! Bonjour la classe. Bonjour Madame, ça va? Oui, ça va bien merci. Asseyez-vous.* Choral responses are ideal as they give an immediate opportunity for children to speak the language and bring the class together, but with no pressure to 'perform' individually. Alternatively, counting round the class or responding to the register in a particular way works well. As learners develop more language, vary the starter, but keep it basic and familiar to ensure that all children can participate. More able children might lead the choral responses, but the starter should be more reassuring than challenging.

Your starter provides an opportunity to revisit prior learning and gain an idea about how the class and individuals within it have assimilated past work. At the end of your starter, you may find that you need to alter slightly your planned lesson, especially if your new input relies on using previously taught vocabulary.

## Main

As you can see from the QCA schemes of work, the main part of your lesson is likely to include a variety of activities linked to your objectives. How many there are and the form they take depends, in part, on the length of your lesson. It is important that you **fit your activities to your learning objectives and not the other way round**.

Ask yourself: 'How can I best organise and teach the class to achieve my learning objectives?'

Having a plan enables you to introduce activities logically. In our discussion of oracy and literacy in Chapter 4, we saw that the initial phase of **exposure** to new words and phrases and **recognition** of their meaning precedes meaningful **production**.

### Presentation, practice and production: (the three Ps)

The suggested lesson plan template therefore incorporates three sub-headings in the box marked Main (see page 57). This is because, in order to ensure coherence in your Primary Languages lesson, you need to think about three stages, the first two of which we began to consider in Chapter 4 when we were reflecting on repetition and question and answer work. These are:

- **presentation**, when you expose children to the new language and introduce new vocabulary or a new structure as part of a varied repetition and graded question and answer phase;
- **practice**, when children have the opportunity to take the new language they have been introduced to a bit further and practise it in game-like and pair work activities;
- **production**, when children use the new structure or vocabulary for themselves. This latter phase may not occur in every lesson, but at some point during a unit of work you should provide opportunities for children to work independently, using the new language without prompting from the teacher.

Short circuiting this process by asking children to produce too much language too soon can be threatening and make children anxious about being 'put on the spot'. You can overcome this to some extent by asking for volunteers instead of targeting questions at nominated children. However, be aware that often the same enthusiastic children tend to volunteer and you must therefore plan for all children to engage in some individual speaking, so that all have a chance to use the new language for themselves.

Although gradual exposure to new language is one way in, children need to hear and see blocks of language to use as a model for their own utterances, which is why the rhythm in songs, rhymes and story texts makes them an extremely effective means of enabling many children to internalise sentence structures. You can find numerous examples of age appropriate activities, which match children's level of cognitive development and offer them opportunities to apply their learning in the trainee support materials/QCA schemes of work.

**PRACTICAL TASK** PRACTICAL TASK PRACTICAL TASK PRACTICAL TASK PRACTICAL TASK

(You need your QCA schemes of work Teacher's Guide or your tutor may wish to copy pages 17/18.) Using the section entitled Presentation on pages 17/18, note the suggestions for teaching strategies.

- Underline the Presentation ideas you have observed, and tick any you have actually tried yourself.
- Decide on at least one to incorporate in your next Primary Languages lesson plan.

### Practice

Once key vocabulary has been introduced or revised using a variety of strategies, children need the opportunity to consolidate in smaller groups/pairs. This allows children to process the new language and make their own sense of it. As we saw in Chapter 4, early language lessons are weighted towards choral repetition, total physical response and group activities, with lots of listening and responding. Additionally, most lessons should allow children some 'breathing space' to practise the language at their own pace with a talk partner.

**PRACTICAL TASK** PRACTICAL TASK PRACTICAL TASK PRACTICAL TASK PRACTICAL TASK

(You need your QCA schemes of work for Key Stage 2.)

Consider carefully the sequence of teaching activities under the heading Main in either Unit 10, *Our sporting lives* or another unit of your choice.

- Look to see which learning objectives from the Key Stage Framework are being addressed by the activities and how they fit into the 3Ps sequence.

### Production

Factors such as the age of the children and the length of time they have been learning the new language affects the complexity of the structures you teach. As we shall see in Chapter 7 on progression, chunks of language learned as a whole are a very useful device in the early stages of learning a language, because they enable children to communicate with each other and the teacher immediately. However, you also need to encourage learners to create sentences for themselves. So, returning to the sports theme, your learners might develop their sentences along the following lines:

- I go swimming.
- I go swimming **and** I do skateboarding.
- I **like** going swimming and I **love skateboarding.**
- I like swimming **but** I **prefer** skateboarding.
- I like swimming but I prefer skateboarding **because** it is cool.

The QCA schemes of work includes a whole range of exciting suggestions for production activities, some of which are not just end-of-lesson but end-of-unit, such as performances within an assembly, presentations to other classes or to the learner's own class, songs, stories and poems.

**PRACTICAL TASK** PRACTICAL TASK **PRACTICAL TASK** PRACTICAL TASK **PRACTICAL TASK**

(You will need your QCA schemes of work Teacher's Guide page 19.)

- Brainstorm some ideas for production activities.
- Compare your suggestions with those on page 19 under the heading Production.

## Target language

The lesson template on page 56 provides space to note the actual target language that you are going to use for different purposes during the lesson. However fluent you personally are, and this applies to native speakers too, it is vital to really think through the target language you are going to use, especially when you are setting up activities or giving instructions for game-like activities. It helps if you script what you are going to say in a step-by-step way. General principles are as follows.

- Plan and prepare your target language.
- Make sure you have the class's full attention. You need phrases like: *Attention. Posez les crayons. Regardez-moi. Ecoutez.*
- Be brief and simple.
- Give the instructions in short, discrete sections.
- Emphasise key words and slow delivery.
- Model what you want to happen.
- Give examples and demonstrate.
- Use visual clues, deliberate gestures.
- Be prepared to present information more than once.
- Monitor understanding as you go along.

The QCA trainee support materials have regrouped the language you may need in the classroom into core language, plus teacher language and pupil language. Use this guidance as a starting point when planning how to manage the classroom in the new language.

## Assessment for learning

At the point at which we are planning our Primary Languages lessons, we need to bear in mind assessment opportunities, particularly those for AfL or formative assessment. Hence the template suggests you mark any activity which provides an assessment opportunity with an A. (This saves you writing out the assessment opportunities in full somewhere else.)

> *Assessment for learning is the process of seeking and interpreting evidence for use by learners and their teachers to decide, where the learners are in their learning, where they need to go, and how best to get there.*
>
> (Assessment Reform Group, 2002, p2)

AfL is any assessment activity which serves to inform the next steps to learning. Ask yourself, 'How can I check during my lesson how well children are understanding and learning?'

A key area in AfL as we saw, is:

● sharing the learning objectives.

In addition, further features of AfL are:

● effective questioning;
● feedback;
● peer and self-assessment;
● thoughtful, confident, active learners.

Whilst you are teaching, monitor children's understanding by looking and listening to their responses, both physical and verbal. Watch to see how children are participating in games. Give formative oral feedback, particularly when they are answering questions in the new language. You can do this by modelling the correct response if children do not quite respond as they should.

An informal *Ça va? Oui ou non?* with a show of thumbs up or down provides an indicator of when children are ready to move on. When you ask for thumbs up, suggest that children put up one thumb and keep it close to their chest. This avoids lots of waving thumbs in the air and makes the self-assessment less threatening.

You can ask the class as a whole: *Tout le monde comprend? Vous comprenez?* However, do not rely on blanket questions. Ask individuals: *Tu comprends, Scott? Ça va, Sarah?* Ask other children to act as the class interpreter and explain for the rest: *Qui peut expliquer?*

Some teachers use various versions of traffic lighting: green lights indicate full understanding, amber, some understanding, and red that the learner does not understand at all. Others use a 'smiley face' system against various learning objectives.

Black and Wiliam make the following recommendation:

> *For formative assessment to be productive, pupils need to be trained in self-assessment so that they can understand the main purposes of their learning and thereby grasp what they need to do to achieve.*
>
> (1998, p10)

Explore which of the systems for peer and self-assessment that your school operates for other foundation subjects can be adapted for use in your Primary Languages lessons.

**PRACTICAL TASK** PRACTICAL TASK PRACTICAL TASK PRACTICAL TASK PRACTICAL TASK

Access the Primary Languages Training zone at www.primarylanguages.org.uk. Go to Using the Key Stage 2 Framework. Select Assessing and recording, and peer assessment. Here you will see a German teacher helping children to use two stars and a wish to peer assess whether they can meet the learning intentions for the lesson.

- Have you seen this system being used in Primary Languages lessons or in other curriculum areas?
- How does the teacher guide the children to carry out the peer assessment correctly?
- Share with other trainees what you have observed about how teachers give feedback.

AfL focuses on learning how to learn and in this respect is linked to the Language Learning Strategies strand of the Framework. We consider Language Learning Strategies again in Chapter 7 on continuity and progression.

**REFLECTIVE TASK**

Explore with your mentors how to encourage children to recognise that **how** they learn is as important as **what** they learn.

# Plenary

You will notice that the lesson proforma on page 61 includes approximate timings for each segment of the lesson. This is because it is essential to plan-in the plenary and allow at least 5 minutes for it. It is better to omit one activity earlier on and allow sufficient time for the plenary rather than rush at the end and not have enough time. Why is a plenary so important?

AfL often occurs, though not exclusively, during the plenary when you give children an opportunity to reflect on what they have learned in the course of the lesson. This reflection may take different forms but should include reference to the learning objectives. In the plenary you might ask:

- Can you do this?
- How many sports can you name? (for example)
- How confident are you?
- What did we have to do to be successful?

A plenary offers children a chance to take stock of their learning and for you to guide them in consolidating their understanding. Children should leave a lesson knowing what they have learned. Self-assessment is a thinking and talking activity and a skill, in which children need to be trained (Pollard, 2005), which implies that you should not let the target language get in the way of making the learning clear.

In the words of Clarke, who suggests displaying a range of self-evaluative questions:

> A major part of the plenary of a lesson should be children's reflective commentary about their learning, followed by teacher summary, unravelling misconceptions and providing links with future learning.

> (2001, p57)

# After the lesson

## Using your lesson plan as a record

**REFLECTIVE TASK**

How will you ensure that you actually **use** the information gained from the assessment for learning.

It is helpful to consider your short-term plans as working documents. If you annotate them after delivering your lesson and briefly note children's responses they can become useful records. On the lesson template adjacent to the learning objectives is a space for you to note down names of children who have exceeded expectations and those who struggled to meet the learning objectives. When it comes to your next lesson, you can assume that children whose names are *not* listed achieved the learning objectives and are probably ready to move on.

## Self-evaluation

Your lesson plans, together with the learning objectives and the notes you have made, will provide you with a basis for reflection after the lesson. You might find it helpful to consider the following prompts when you review your lessons:

- Did I achieve my learning objectives?
- What did children learn?
- How do I know?
- Did each child perform as anticipated?
- Who needs support?
- Who needs challenging?
- Action for next time.

If you do this carefully over a series of lessons, and discuss your reflections with your mentor and university tutor, you will find that you make progress in:

- the appropriateness of the learning objectives you devise;
- the suitability of the activities;
- your presentation and practice of new language;
- your explanations and questioning.

**PRACTICAL TASK** PRACTICAL TASK **PRACTICAL TASK** PRACTICAL TASK **PRACTICAL TASK**

**Planning a lesson**

(You need your QCA scheme of work and/or trainee support materials.)

As a group of trainees, divide into pairs. Each pair should select a unit from the scheme of work, preferably a different unit per pair. Decide with your tutor whether you will take an aspect of the unit you chose for the segment in Chapter 4, page 38 or whether you will choose a different one.

- Each pair should then select a **section of the unit** and use it to plan a 30-minute lesson, using the template as a guide.
- Share your plans with each other and pool ideas.

(If you are soon to be on placement or are in school, relate this planning to a real lesson with real children.)

## A SUMMARY OF **KEY POINTS**

> Locate individual lessons in the context of a medium-term plan/unit of work.

> Medium-term plans should be part of a scheme of work or long-term plan.

> Build on children's prior knowledge.

> Using a lesson template for Primary Languages lessons helps ensure that lessons have a clear structure: a beginning, middle and end.

> Lesson objectives need to be precise and expressed clearly.

> Lesson objectives should be shared with learners.

> Lesson objectives should be revisited at the end of the lesson in the plenary.

> A starter should be both familiar and stimulating.

> New language is often presented, practised and produced, but you may not cover all these stages within a single lesson.

> A variety of activities should cater for children's preferred learning styles.

> AfL is integral to effective lesson planning.

> Try not to omit a final plenary to review learning.

> Time spent planning and preparing will enable you to teach more confidently as you will know what is 'coming next' in your lessons.

**MOVING** *ON* > > > > > > MOVING *ON* > > > > > > MOVING *ON*

Thorough planning and preparation are at the heart of excellent Primary Languages lessons. Continue to plan in as much detail as possible. This will give you confidence when you come to deliver your lessons and will help avoid behaviour management issues and improve pace. Continue to familiarise yourself with the Key Stage 2 Framework for Languages and the QCA schemes of work for Key Stage 2 languages.

**FURTHER READING** FURTHER READING **FURTHER READING** FURTHER READING

Jones, J. and Coffey, S. (2006) Assessment and monitoring progress: How am I doing? What have I achieved? How can I progress? in Jones, J. and Coffey, S. *Modern foreign languages 5–11*. London: David Fulton Publishers. This provides more practical strategies for AfL.

# Useful website

www.assessment-reform-group.org/ – Assessment Reform Group

# 6

# Exploring the notion of Intercultural Understanding

*Language competence and* Intercultural Understanding *are an essential part of being a citizen. Children develop a greater understanding of their own lives in the* context of exploring the lives of others. They learn to look at things from another's perspective, *giving them insight into the people, culture and traditions of other cultures. Children become more aware of the similarities and differences between peoples, their daily lives, beliefs and values.*

(DfES, 2005, Part 1:1 p8 [my emphasis])

## By the end of this chapter you will have:

- **briefly explored the notion of communicative competence;**
- **considered Intercultural Understanding within the communicative language teaching model;**
- **reflected on what it means to be an intercultural speaker;**
- **explored practical ideas for developing Intercultural Understanding in children using the Key Stage 2 Framework and the QCA schemes of work for languages;**
- **appreciated the importance of developing your own interculturality through reflection on your teaching placement or any experience abroad;**
- **appreciated the opportunity to make connections between other curriculum areas such as citizenship, PSHE, ICT, music, art and languages.**

This chapter addresses the following Professional Standards for QTS:
**Q14, Q15, Q23, Q25a, Q32**

This chapter explores the concept of Intercultural Understanding from the perspective of young language learners and how we might begin to develop Intercultural Understanding in schools. It also considers what Intercultural Understanding might involve for adults, such as teacher trainees or teachers spending time abroad. We start by placing Intercultural Understanding within a theoretical rationale and then consider the Intercultural Understanding strand within the non-statutory Key Stage 2 Framework and the new QCA schemes of work for languages in Key Stage 2. Finally, we look at developing our own intercultural competence by means of a stay abroad. The appendix on page 141 offers further practical suggestions for activities to do with children related to Intercultural Understanding.

## REFLECTIVE TASK

Are **you** in a position to teach the Intercultural Understanding content suggested in the Key Stage 2 Framework? Ask yourself these questions drawn from the Intercultural Understanding strand of the Framework.

- Are you aware of linguistic and cultural diversity?

- Do you know about dialects/accents and some different languages?
- Do you know the social conventions of your own and some other cultures?
- Do you have contact with native speakers or schools abroad?
- Are you aware of authentic TV/video/internet provision?
- Do you recognise diversity within cultures in the ways in which they celebrate festivals?
- Do you know some traditional tales, songs, poems, dances in the target language?
- Do you know the location and geography of the countries where the target language is spoken?
- Have you stayed in a foreign country/with a family?
- Are you able to recognise and challenge stereotypes?

(Skarbek, 2008)

# Towards a theoretical framework for Intercultural Understanding

Intercultural Understanding is one of the dimensions of **communicative competence**. The term communicative competence describes the system of rules and strategies that learners must be able to operate, if they are to use a language for communication. So let us start by considering what it means to be competent in a foreign language.

## REFLECTIVE TASK

Read the section in Johnstone, 1994, *Teaching Modern Languages in Primary School* (pp22–25) on communicative competence.

- What does it mean to be competent in a language?
- What skills do we need?
- With reference to your allocated section from the reading, sum up in your own words with any examples you can think of, the knowledge and skills required to be competent.
- Present your section to the others in the group.
- Taken together, what are the elements which make up communicative competence?

Communicative competence has been described by other researchers, notably Canale (1983), a Canadian, as having four components. The first of these is:

- **grammatical competence** (the knowledge of grammar and dictionary meanings of vocabulary and the ability to understand and produce grammatically correct language).

Grammatical or linguistic competence has traditionally been considered as all a language speaker needs in order to communicate effectively. However, you will be aware that even people who can produce grammatically correct sentences do not always choose language which is completely appropriate to the occasion and may, in fact, not be communicating very well. Grammatical competence on its own is therefore insufficient. Communicative competence needs to include other elements such as:

- **sociolinguistic competence** (the ability to understand language in a specific social context);

- **discourse competence** (the ability to clarify and negotiate to overcome difficulties in understanding or production);
- **strategic competence** (knowing how to get round gaps in one's knowledge of the target language and overcome difficulties in communication, mainly brought about through incomplete knowledge of the language).

As a language learner, you will find that the development of the final three competences listed above will help you speak appropriately and choose language which suits the occasion, the topic and the person with whom you are speaking (your interlocutor).

In the late 1980s, a fifth component, **(inter)cultural competence**, was added. However, language learning theories still viewed (inter)cultural competence and the study of culture as a **support** to the main task of language learning and becoming linguistically proficient.

---

**REFLECTIVE TASK**

**Intercultural understanding – why do we need it?**

Before we consider further what it means to be interculturally competent, pause for a moment and discuss in your group why it is so important to develop intercultural awareness.

- Is learning a language sufficient?
- What kind of society are our learners growing up into in the twenty-first century?
- What kinds of aims are often proposed for Primary Languages programmes?
- Do any of these relate to intercultural understanding?
- Ask someone to act as scribe for you and keep a note of the group's responses. You may wish to return to them later in the chapter.

---

# Intercultural Understanding – have you got it? Developing your own intercultural awareness

An eminent writer on intercultural competence, Michael Byram of Durham University, suggests that early formulations of communicative competence such as Hymes (1971) are based on an analysis of how *native speakers* interact with each other. According to Byram this theory needs to be extended to encompass either a *non-native speaker* of a language speaking to a native speaker, or *two non-native speakers* communicating *using the foreign language as a lingua franca, as it is the language which they both have in common.* In the past, even when one of the speakers was **not** a native speaker, it was assumed that their ultimate aim was to become as like a native speaker as possible.

Whenever you interact socially with someone from a different country, you bring to the situation your knowledge of the world. For some of you who may have lived, studied, worked or spent holidays abroad, this may include a substantial knowledge of the country in question. For others of you who are preparing to teach a new language and its culture to children but have not yet had much contact with the country and its speakers, this may be quite limited. Nonetheless, both of you bring to the interaction your knowledge of your own country and may also share with your interlocutor one or more of your social identities. For example, when some of you go abroad on your school experience placement, you will share a professional identity with your buddy teacher trainees in the host country.

The native speaker has knowledge which is internalised and unconscious but which the foreign language learner has to know consciously and, in some situations, substitute for their own unconscious knowledge. Native speakers also have conscious knowledge acquired through formal education and the informal channels of media and social interaction.

Byram and Zarate (1997) have suggested that rather than attempting to become like a native speaker, the language learner needs to acquire attitudes, knowledge and skills of an *intercultural speaker*. In your own university sessions relating language learning theories to practice, you may have discussed how to set up pair work activities between children which have an 'information gap' – in other words, children genuinely have to try to find something out which is not obvious, or one partner has one set of information and the other a different one. In this case, the exchange of information, getting the message across, is important and when this happens, the interaction is deemed to be successful. However, Byram and Zarate stress that success criteria for effective communication should also include to what extent human relationships have been established or maintained. Developing interpersonal understanding depends on attitudinal factors, including being willing to anticipate problems of communication caused by a lack of overlap in knowledge of the world and of each other's country.

The knowledge you are likely to bring to an interaction with someone from another country may be dominated by the notion of a national culture and identity. These, together with other regional, ethnic and social class identities, are acquired through formal and informal socialisation. The knowledge you have of the shared beliefs, meanings and behaviours of these different groups includes a **conscious awareness** of characteristics which are emblematic for the group, for example modes of greeting or dress, and those which it uses to differentiate it from other groups such as stories from its history. Many of these characteristics are taken for granted and you may not become consciously aware of them until you begin to contrast them with those in other groups.

Knowledge about other countries and how the inhabitants perceive another country is **relational**. Knowledge of the history of another country is through the stories – often stereotyped – from the history of the nation state and is a **different** interpretation from the one within the foreign country. An awareness that you are a product of your own socialisation is a precondition for understanding your reactions to otherness. Similarly, awareness that your 'natural' ways of interacting with other people are the 'naturalised' product of socialisation, and how parallel but different modes of interaction can be expected in other cultures, is part of the knowledge an intercultural speaker needs.

## The five *savoirs*

Thus, Byram and Doyé (1999, p141) suggest that if you are an intercultural speaker, you need particular attitudes, knowledge and skills. (You will see that each has a French term related to it.)

**REFLECTIVE TASK**

Read Byram and Doyé, 1999 pp140–143. What attitudes, knowledge and skills does an intercultural speaker require? Copy and complete the grid below using the chapter extract as a guide.

**Attitudes, knowledge, skills**

- *savoir être*
- *savoirs* = knowledge
- *savoir comprendre*
- *savoir apprendre/faire*
- *savoir s'engager*

- **Attitudes** (*savoir être*): **curiosity and openness**, a **willingness** to accept the **other person's perspective as normal** and one's own as strange when seen from the other's perspective, a readiness to suspend disbelief about other cultures and belief about one's own judgement with respect to others' meanings, beliefs and behaviours.
- **Knowledge** (*savoirs*): of different social groups in one's own society and that of one's foreign interlocutor, of their cultural practices and products and of the social processes involved when people of different groups or societies interact.
- **Skills** of interpreting and relating (*savoir comprendre*): the **ability to use knowledge of one's own and the other society** to interpret.
- **Skills** of **discovery** and **interaction** (*savoir apprendre/faire*}: the ability to acquire new knowledge about one's interlocutor and to interact with them under real time pressures.
- *savoir s'engager*: the development of learners' critical cultural awareness.

Clearly, much of the descriptors above refers to more mature learners, who have been learning a language for a considerable time with quite substantial life experience. Nevertheless, there may be elements of some of the *savoirs* which are appropriate for the primary phase and others more suitable for yourselves as trainees, some of whom will participate in the placement abroad. Nonetheless, jot down which might be relevant for young children and which for much older learners ... we shall come back to this question later in the chapter (see page 80).

Reviewing past approaches to school-based language teaching in the secondary phase, Byram (1989) notes that traditionally there has been an emphasis in cultural learning on the acquisition of information about another country in the form of decontextualised facts.

# What intercultural understanding is not

However, in a conference presentation Skarbek cautions that intercultural understanding does *not* mean:

> simply teaching children lots of **facts** about a foreign country, especially when those selected just serve to accentuate difference and do not enhance under-standing.
>
> (2005)

Indeed, if language learning is largely limited to simply that, learning the *language*, and the teaching of culture is 'intuitive and unsystematic', then:

- learners will acquire some *information* but very little *knowledge* of the foreign culture
- there is a difference between *information* and *knowledge*
- even increased *knowledge* does not necessarily create *positive attitudes*.

In the words of Byram:

*An unsystematic approach to providing information leaves pupils precisely with unstructured information rather than knowledge*

(1989, p120)

## REFLECTIVE TASK

This means that as Primary Languages teachers, we must **plan our cultural input** at least as thoroughly as we plan our **language input**. But how should we go about it? What criteria should we use to select cultural topics for introduction to children?

## REFLECTIVE TASK

**Some important questions relating to children's psychological development**

Using what you have been discovering about young children's development in the rest of your initial teacher training programme, discuss in small groups the following questions:

- At what age/stage of affective and attitudinal development should we begin to introduce cultural awareness through raising awareness of similarities and differences?
- Should we have different aims for different age groups?
- At what point are learners likely to be able to 'decentre' and view their own culture objectively from 'a distance'?

Interestingly, Piaget and Weil (1951, cited in Byram, 1994) suggested that before children can acquire an understanding of their own country, they must be able to decentre and understand points of view different from their own. Three stages are suggested:

- **egocentricity**: when what learners say about their own and other countries is arbitrary and based on momentary preferences;
- **sociocentricity**: when learners express opinions reflecting the views of their immediate social environment;
- **reciprocity**: when learners have reached the point of perceiving other people's views of themselves and begin to realise that they themselves may be viewed as 'foreigners'.

Remember though, that these ages and stages are not fixed and slippage can occur in both directions, with children sometimes moving back into a previous stage. The optimistic Piagetian view of young secondary school children reaching a stage of reciprocity and being able to decentre must be treated with caution (Byram, 1994, p19).

Another writer (Wiegand, 1992 cited in Byram, 1994) discusses primary children's understanding of space and place and their sense of their own national identity and national symbols. He points out that young learners find conceptualising relationships between geographical units difficult, for example that towns are within counties and counties within countries and countries within continents. In fact, primary age children are still very much in the process of acquiring adult perceptions of themselves and their country (see Table 6.1 Wiegand, 1992, p54 in Byram, 1994). Certainly as language teachers we need to be aware that our younger children may not yet have a fully developed conception of the country whose language they are learning.

**Table 6.1 From Wiegand, 1992, p54 in Byram, 1994**

| Generalised level of development | Children are generally found to |
|---|---|
| *I Age 6–8* | *Have no understanding of part–whole relationships (e.g. Glasgow–Scotland–Britain) and prefer their own country but for no rational reason* |
| *II age 7–9* | *Have imperfect understanding of part–whole relationships, and prefer their own country for family and immediate social reasons* |
| *III age 9–11* | *Understand part–whole relationships, prefer their own country by reference to collective ideals and recognise and understand the significance of national symbols* |

# Attitudes

In the primary school we are concerned as much with the **complex processes of attitude formation as with attitude change**, with relationships between the cognitive and affective components of attitudes towards other peoples, between information and the way in which it is presented, between general psychological development and specific development of perceptions of foreign and native cultures and countries. In your discussion about the aims of Primary Languages programmes (see Chapter 2) some of you may have mentioned 'developing positive attitudes' or 'promoting tolerance' or even 'combating prejudice and stereotypes'. It is noteworthy, however, that **simply exposing children to language learning or to other cultures, will not, of itself, lead to any of these outcomes**.

Before learning about other countries, many children are neither positively nor negatively disposed towards the countries in question. According to Wiegand (1992), *they simply haven't thought about them at all and don't have any clearly developed view* (see Table 6.2).

It is important to note that simply developing 'positive attitudes' is not sufficient for successful intercultural communication.

**Table 6.2. From Wiegand, 1992, p58, in Byram, 1994**

| Generalised level of development | Children generally found to |
|---|---|
| *I age 6–8* | *Select favourite countries on the basis of exotic features, stress differences between themselves and foreigners, deny that they themselves could become 'foreigners'* |
| *II age 7–9* | *Select favourite countries on the basis of stereotypes, have an imperfect understanding of the concept foreigner* |
| *III age 9–10* | *Accept more similarities between themselves and other peoples, are increasingly able to see the point of view of other peoples, understand that foreigners are people out of their own country* |

# Some guidelines for choosing cultural themes

We should try to ensure that:

- activities and experiences are in line with the **children's developmental stage** (what Byram calls *learner appropriateness*);
- examples reflect real, contemporary life: our starting point should be children's **own environment**;
- children **begin by looking at the lives of children of the same age** living in different countries and at the habits, symbols, rituals and artefacts that constitute their cultural life;
- we present a **variety of perspectives**;
- children understand that there is **more than one set of beliefs**, meanings and behaviours in any one country;
- **we avoid generalisations** which give the impression that a specific image can be generalised to the **whole society** and culture in question;
- we **beware of presenting a culture as if it were unchanging over time**;
- we use **authentic materials** and **images** in our portrayal of the foreign country, including information about a range of social classes and ethnic groups, different kinds of family structure, different employment and unemployment situations.

The important thing for us as primary language teachers is that by encouraging children to compare foreign behaviours, beliefs and meanings by contrast with their own, we lead them to begin the process of **evaluating their own culture** as well as the culture of the target language country.

# Developing Intercultural Understanding during the primary phase

*Younger children naturally have a keen curiosity and a flexible adaptable mind which makes them such good intercultural language learners.*

(Jones and Coffey, 2006, p142)

Byram and Doyé (1999) are also of the view that the foundations for intercultural competence can be laid within the primary school, since primary age children already possess some *savoirs* (knowledge) of their own social group's practices. Indeed, *savoir être*, the attitude of openness and curiosity, seems especially suited to the primary phase.

Since their chapter was written in 1999, there have been major developments within the field of Primary Languages in the UK. These started in the same year that Byram and Doyé were writing, when the non-statutory guidelines for modern foreign languages were included for the first time in the Primary National Curriculum Handbook, with the statement under knowledge, skills and understanding that:

*Pupils may be taught about other countries and cultures by*
- *working with authentic materials including some from ICT based resources*
- *considering their own culture and comparing it with others*
- *considering the experiences of other people.*

(DfEE/QCA, 1999b, p143)

Currently the most significant development has been the incorporation of Intercultural Understanding as a major third strand, alongside Oracy and Literacy, within the Key Stage 2 Framework for Languages (DfES, 2005).

Jones and Coffey (2006) sum up possible stages as follows:

- *The **input phase**: when there is interaction with the new culture and language*
- *A phase of **comparison** between the two*
- *A **reassessment** of the initial position.*

(2006, p138)

# Intercultural understanding in the Key Stage 2 Framework for Languages

## REFLECTIVE TASK

(You will need your Key Stage 2 Framework or a photocopy of Part 1, p75.)

Read Byram and Doyé, 1999, pp143–46. Having done so, consider the Expectations and Outcomes for Intercultural Understanding summarised in the overview on page 75.

Use a highlighter pen to indicate key words.

What do you notice about how the suggestions for raising children's awareness of other languages and cultures develop over the four years between Year 3 and Year 6? What are the starting points and how do children progress?

## PRACTICAL TASK PRACTICAL TASK PRACTICAL TASK PRACTICAL TASK PRACTICAL TASK

(You will need access to the Primary Languages Training Zone at www.primarylanguages.org.uk.)

Go to Using the Key Stage 2 Framework and select Intercultural Understanding. Here you will see six extracts.

- View each extract and discuss the way in which these activities fulfil the requirements identified by Byram and Doyé.

- Have you observed any similar activities with young language learners in schools you have trained in?

First of all we need to note that intercultural understanding within the Key Stage 2 Framework is **not intended to be taught solely within language lessons**. As the Framework states:

> *There are many opportunities to link this strand with work in other subjects. Objectives in this strand can be integrated into language lessons as well as taught separately in non-language teaching time, through other subjects.*

(DfES, 2005, Part 1:1 p8)

Here are some examples taken from other curriculum areas:

> *Read stories from other cultures by focusing on e.g. differences in place, time, customs, relationships; to identify and discuss recurring themes where appropriate*

(National Literacy Strategy Year 4 T3 T2)

*To listen to a range of live and recorded music from different times and cultures*
(National Curriculum, Music 5e)

*To learn about the social, cultural, religious and ethnic diversity of the societies studied, in Britain and the wider world*
(National Curriculum, History 2b)

The Framework for personal, social and health education (PSHE) and citizenship at Key Stages 1 and 2 was introduced into schools in 2000 and has since become an important part of the non-statutory areas of the National Curriculum in primary schools. So, for example, we find the following:

*To think about the lives of people living in other places and times and people with different values and customs*
(National Curriculum, PSHE 4b)

Traditionally, classroom-based language learning has been viewed as 'preparation for the real world' or 'for the future' but this view is outdated. As Jones and Coffey point out:

*In urban areas children live with difference all around them. In other schools where the ethnic cultural make up of the school is homogenous, intercultural awareness is all the more important... Intercultural Understanding has the potential to steer children away from a restrictive monocultural, monolingual view of the world.*
(2006, p137)

In the words of Brown:

*Language teachers are well placed to help pupils learn about and understand diversity in the United Kingdom and develop an awareness of cultural diversity in the countries which speak the language they are learning.*
(2003, p83)

The Key Stage 2 Framework therefore suggests children begin in Year 3:

- by acknowledging linguistic and cultural diversity within their own family, school and community through descriptions of children's own lives, languages and traditions (summed up by Skarbek, 2005 as the *perspective of self*).

## REFLECTIVE TASK

You may have noticed here that the Framework's starting point with the child's own culture is, in fact, opposite to Piaget's proposition that children need to start by looking at the foreign culture first in order to understand their own.

The Framework moves in Year 4 on to:

- A raising of awareness of similarities and differences between cultures, with a focus on festivals, special days, celebrations and aspects of the child's everyday life. (The consideration of the **relationship between cultures** implies a comparative approach: the key word here being 'compare'.)

By comparing and highlighting similarities and differences in an unbiased manner with the intention of *providing a shared experience* (Jones and Coffey, 2006, p146), learners begin to **relativise** their own perspectives on things they have taken for granted. They gradually move from perception of these similarities and differences towards **accepting other people's perspectives**, and valuing them as equally acceptable within their own terms. Seeing their own culture and society through other people's perspectives is a means of bringing unconscious and naturalised beliefs into consciousness, so that their relativity and specificity can be acknowledged. This process may (much) later on lead to critical distancing and decentring from them (Byram, 1994, p177).

In Year 5 children:

- begin to **imagine what it might be like to be a foreigner**, as they look at objects, realia, symbols and products (summed up by Skarbek, 2005 as the *other perspective*).

And finally, older primary learners in Year 6 present information about an aspect of another culture, share and justify opinions. They begin to understand the link between language, culture and personal identity – the *objective perspective* (Skarbek, 2005). So doing, encourages reflexivity and thinking about their immediate experience and makes children aware of the specificity of their own culture.

In summary, children's experiences need to be:

- concrete;
- experiential;
- systematically arranged;
- built upon their prior and current experiences and knowledge of symbols, practices and products.

So how might we raise cultural awareness in children using activities linked to the Key Stage 2 Framework? Let's begin with the first objective from Year 3: Learn about the different languages spoken by children in the school (IU 3.1).

---

### CLASSROOM STORY

Here are some suggestions from Louise, a primary teacher:
Record an interview (like a radio interview) with one child about the languages the child can speak or understand.
Follow up with investigating where in the world the language is used.
Make cross-curricular links with maths – for example, graphs and charts of how many children in school speak which languages.

(Pagden, 2008)

If you turn to the QCA schemes of work Unit 1 in either French, German or Spanish you will see that this objective also links with PSHE:
- develop good relationships and respect differences between people;
- appreciate that differences and similarities between people arise from a number of factors;
- listen to other people;
- play and work cooperatively.

(IU 3.1, IU 3.2)

---

PRACTICAL TASK PRACTICAL TASK PRACTICAL TASK PRACTICAL TASK PRACTICAL TASK

**Intercultural Understanding in the QCA schemes of work**

Allocate a QCA unit in the language of your choice to each of the members of your group.

- Each of you should identify **where** intercultural understanding is introduced within the selected unit and **which** IU objectives are being addressed.

- Note down the teaching ideas.

- Suggest alternatives of your own.

- Collaboratively compile a list of ideas for the whole group to use.

# Empathy and imagination

Empathy can be viewed as the notion of placing oneself in someone else's shoes.

*It is crucial that pupils attempt to* imagine what it would be like *to be someone different.*

(Byram 1994, p29 [my emphasis])

Hawkins (1981; 1996) has indicated that many children's capacity for empathy or ability to see the world from someone else's point of view is at its best around the age of nine, but declines rapidly with the onset of adolescence. After puberty, he says, attitudes become increasingly fixed and it is more difficult to tackle issues of difference.

Significantly, the teacher is crucial for the development of empathy, both as a source of information and as a model.

If you are a trainee on the Primary Languages Initial Teacher Training project your HEI will be partnered with a teacher training institution in the target language country and that institution will be sending its own trainees to England on school experience. These young native speaker teacher trainees (along with Foreign Language Assistants and other native speakers) can be the means of providing useful and relevant cultural exposure to children in partnership primary schools. Contact with native speakers is recognised as an important aspect of integrative motivation (Gardner and Lambert, 1972; Schumann, 1978).

Reporting on an early innovative project which deployed young native speakers for French, German and Spanish in primary schools, Mitchell, Martin and Grenfell (1992) suggest that if learners develop a genuine empathy towards the country and its people through such personal contacts, it is likely that they will develop positive attitudes towards learning the language. Furthermore, as we saw above, Hawkins (1996) states that the capacity for empathy declines with the onset of adolescence. It thus makes sense to capitalise on young children's acceptance of differences in others and openness to the unfamiliar.

Providing opportunities for cultural development and broadening children's understanding of their own culture as well as that of others has implications for the teacher's own cultural knowledge. Primary Languages teachers need to be able to access relevant cultural information and step outside their own culture in order to gain a fresh perspective. Doyé (1995) suggests that **teachers themselves need to be intercultural learners**, so that they can see cultural variables side by side. Furthermore, the more credible the presenter, the more acceptable is the message and this is where having had **personal experience within the foreign culture** is so valuable. Having been there yourself not only gives you 'street cred' but sets an example at the same time. Indeed, Byram and Doyé (1999) stress that primary teachers who incorporate intercultural understanding within their own language teaching require **substantial intercultural competence themselves**. They propose that all Primary Languages teacher trainees should have a period of residence in another country. However, residence in the foreign country does not in itself guarantee the acquisition of cultural knowledge and understanding (Byram, 1994, p62). It is vital to develop and reflect on intercultural competence **before, during and after this experience** abroad.

# Making the most of your placement abroad

The final section of this chapter therefore considers ways in which you can make the most of your placement or any period of residence abroad. We shall consider any experience abroad as having four phases:

1. the **preparatory** phase before you go;
2. the phase **while you are abroad**;
3. the **debriefing period** on your return.
4. the **beyond the stay abroad** phase, when you have settled back into your own culture and school and are finding ways to incorporate your experiences into your teaching.

## Tourist versus sojourner

As we saw in our earlier reflection on the elements making up communicative competence, grammatical competence was traditionally considered the most important aim of language teaching and this was displayed in the language examinations of the 1960s, with an emphasis on accurate translation and written composition. However, the move to comprehensive schooling and an increase in the numbers of students aged 11–14 learning a modern language led to new situational syllabuses based on the notion of the language learner as a visitor to the target language country. It was assumed that young learners might go on a day visit as part of a school trip, and once there would want to buy postcards, ice cream and presents to take home. Later they might participate in an exchange and stay with a family, so they would need to introduce themselves, express likes and dislikes, give preferences for food and drink, use the bank, post office or telephones, and perhaps do some travel within the country, using its trains and buses. It was also posited that any visitors coming to the UK from the target language countries would be arriving as tourists. Eventually these scenarios and other similar ones were reflected in GCSE examinations and both learners and their teachers knew the mainly transactional language they would require. However, Byram (1997) has suggested that the role of the tourist is inadequate. Instead the intercultural speaker should be:

- willing to engage with otherness in a relationship of equality, rather than looking for exotic experiences (the 'tourist' approach);
- ready to experience the different stages of adaptation to another culture during a period of residence;
- able to cope with their own different kinds of experience of otherness (enthusiasm, withdrawal) during residence and place them in a longer-term context of phases of acceptance and rejection.

Even though your placement will only be four weeks, and as such of relatively short duration, you need to be aware that living and working abroad involves basic issues of identity.

As you will not be a **tourist** but rather a **sojourner**, you will find yourself having to adapt to different cultural norms and you may find you pass through several stages of adaptation to aspects of the new culture. If you have begun to discuss various cultural expectations prior to departure, as in the brainstorming activity below, some of the culture shock or feelings of bewilderment may be reduced. On the other hand, you still need to be 'open' to whatever you may discover, so as not to spoil the 'wow' factor. However, some kind of culture shock is an almost inevitable part of intercultural learning and growth. Indeed, if your residence is substantial, you may experience:

- an ethnocentric or culture-centric first stage, when you tend to reduce the other to your own code;
- a second stage, when you begin to enter into the cultural code of the other, becoming the other;
- a third stage, as you start to decentre in relationship to cultural codes, your own and that of the other.

You may feel yourself to be more mature and open and end up with a capacity to obtain a distance from your own culture, to see the world from another's point of view, to find it strange and yet not to reject it.

## REFLECTIVE TASK
REFLECTIVE TASK

### Before you go abroad

Here is a reflective task which Christina Skarbek does with her trainees before their departure abroad. *You will need some flipchart or A3 paper and some felt tip markers in different colours.*

- In the centre of each sheet write one key word – home, school, language, culture. Then brainstorm quickly what springs to mind as you think of these words. An extract from a brainstorming sheet completed by trainees visiting the UK can be found on page 86.
- Using the group's responses, do you think you are demonstrating any of the qualities of Byram's intercultural speaker proposed on page 75?
- Discuss your jottings briefly and give them to your tutor to retain for you when you return.

## Reflecting with the Common Reference Framework

If you are part of the TDA multi-lateral ITT project, and particularly if you are teaching in France, Belgium or Germany, you will have a copy of the most recent version of the bilingual *Common Reference Framework*, which has been devised to help scaffold your period abroad. This is a non-statutory document and whether or not you use it in its entirety, it is certainly advisable to consider how best you might exploit opportunities provided by the placement and what your targets might reasonably be. You will have to balance these with work for any other university-based assignments which you need to undertake, either related to your Primary Languages modules or to other curriculum areas.

The *Common Reference Framework* is based on personalised targets and is designed to ensure that you have an opportunity to move progressively from observation to teaching of groups and whole classes in curriculum subjects in the host language and in your own language. There are four sets of spirals relating to:

- professional values;
- pedagogy and practice;
- linguistic competence;
- intercultural understanding.

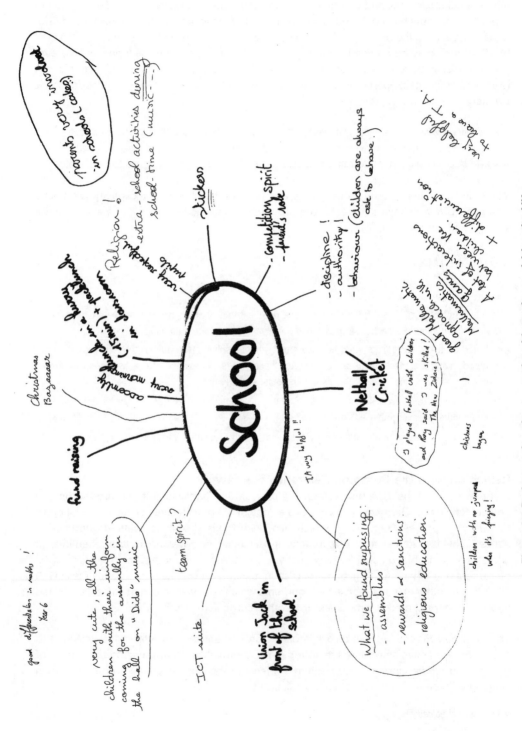

**Figure 6.1 Brainstorming sheet completed by trainees visiting the UK**

## Setting your initial targets

### REFLECTIVE TASK

(You will need your *Common Reference Framework* – go to www.tda.gov.uk/about/publicationslistings/TDA0447.aspx)

Start by reading the statements on each of the four spirals.

- For each of the spirals, decide where you will be starting from (this will vary for each of you in your cohort on account of prior experience, so do not expect to be the same as each other, nor to start at objective 1 necessarily).
- Ask yourself, where you want to get to by the end of the four weeks.
- Write down what you decide on the Initial Target sheet on pages 38–39.
- Be prepared to discuss these targets at your first meeting with your host mentor.

### Whilst abroad

Skarbek (2005) suggests the following guidelines.

- Go with the right attitude – that this will broaden your mind and enhance your perspective.
- Be a sojourner – and make a serious effort to relate to the new culture.
- Immerse yourself by speaking as much in the target language as possible.
- Never say 'no' when given the opportunity to experience cinema, theatre, exhibitions, galleries, museums, local attractions, special occasions.
- Watch TV, listen to the radio, read books, magazines, newspapers, play sport, music, join in.
- Take the opportunity to collect resources for your future teaching, e.g. films, books, stories, poems, songs.

### REFLECTIVE TASK

Keep a brief journal with notes which refer to any cultural experiences you have – use this on your return to help you when reflecting on what you experienced in the foreign country. We suggest that this diary is private and personal and not taken in by a tutor for assessment.

Page 13 of the *Common Reference Framework* states that the placement *provides intercultural development opportunities* and one of the four spirals of objectives is that related to Intercultural Understanding objectives on pages 30–31.

### REFLECTIVE TASK

(You will need your Common Reference Framework.)

Using the **Intercultural Understanding** spirals on pages 30–31, consider each of the prompts under the Observation, Implementation and Evaluation sections.

- When you recall the brainstorm you did before your departure, what strikes you as you observe different features of your placement classroom and school?
- What kinds of similarities and differences are you beginning to identify?
- How are you going to find out the principles and thinking underpinning the teaching styles you are observing?

- What kinds of questions can you ask your host teacher about the way they are interacting with the children?
- What do you notice about the way in which national curricula differ?
- What aspects are similar to the primary National Curriculum for England?

You might like to use the observation tasks provided in Appendix 2 on pages 145–146 to help you to focus your observations.

# On your return

**REFLECTIVE TASK**

**Reflecting on the placement or experience abroad**

(If you did the Reflective task on page 85, ask your tutor for the A3 or flipchart sheets with your pre-placement brainstorm.)

Using your journal, reconsider the notes you made on the themes of home, school, language and culture.

- Were your expectations correct?
- Did things turn out differently from what you anticipated?
- What preconceptions need adjusting in the light of your actual experience?
- Using a different colour cross out things which did not apply after all.
- Add in anything new.
- Discuss your experiences as a group with each other and your tutor.

## Sharing your developing intercultural understanding with others

As we have already mentioned, in order to enable learners to empathise more closely with people of another culture, it is necessary to choose topics relating to the everyday experience of individuals within that culture, at home, at school (if the learners are children), in the workplace (if language learners are adults) and the related social norms and expectations.

**REFLECTIVE TASK**

**After your placement or experience abroad**

- What features of primary school life would you want to share with children as a means of raising their intercultural awareness?

- What features of the professional role of a primary teacher in the target language country would you consider interesting for your teacher colleagues?

- What teaching and assessment practices in the target language country would you consider interesting for your teacher colleagues?

- How would you introduce these characteristics in a presentation to a staff meeting or at a training event for fellow teachers?

- What are teachers' preconceptions likely to be?

> • In preparation for the above, prepare a short, say 10-minute, presentation about your placement/ experience abroad to your fellow (non-language specialist) teacher trainees and tutors. This works best if the postgraduate or undergraduate cohort as a whole is divided into groups of about half a dozen trainees with a tutor. Each trainee who has been on placement abroad then presents to a small group.

By doing the above activity you will be addressing objectives 9 and 10 of the Intercultural Understanding objectives on pages 30–31, namely *compare cultural approaches to primary teaching in the two countries* and *explain and justify, if, when and why you have modified your approach to teaching* (or intend to do so on your next placement).

## Beyond the experience abroad

*Learning a new language inevitably and naturally brings children into contact with aspects of the culture of other countries. The practical nature of language learning may make this contact even more real, whether inside school, on special days or beyond the classroom, by using the internet, e-mail, schools trips abroad and links with other schools.*

(DfES, 2005, Part 1:1 p8)

Here are some further ideas to extend the impact of your placement abroad – remember, good links are built on good relationships.

• Attempt to link up with your placement school/s when you are back in England via email or web cam.
• Try to create a sustainable link for use when you are in post, be it with a foreign trainee, a teacher or a school.

This will give a real purpose to children's writing and enable you to exploit ICT.

*Learn how to share and exchange information in a variety of forms including email.*

(National Curriculum, ICT 3a)

# Celebrating your school's growing intercultural understanding

We finish this chapter with a note about an accreditation scheme for curriculum-based international work in schools, the International Schools Award (ISA). This scheme offers a framework within which to form and develop international partnerships and achieve curriculum goals.

This award encourages and supports schools to develop:

• an international ethos embedded throughout the school;
• involvement of the majority of children within the school in international work;
• collaborative curriculum-based work with a number of partner schools;
• involvement in the wider community;
• evaluation allowing you to improve your activities and your international programme.

A SUMMARY OF **KEY POINTS**

> Intercultural competence is one of five competences which make up communicative competence.

> The intercultural speaker possesses a number of *savoirs*: attitudes, knowledge and skills.

> The first of these, *savoir être*, attitudes of openness, can be nurtured and the development of inter-cultural understanding can start in the primary phase.

> You can incorporate aspects of Intercultural Understanding teaching and learning in language lessons but also in PSHE, citizenship, RE, geography – indeed across the curriculum.

> The Intercultural Understanding strand of the Framework offers children the chance to become more aware of their home culture.

> Learners also have the opportunity to become better informed about issues affecting people in another community in the world.

> This has the potential to challenge taken-for-granted values and preconceptions – including prejudiced views of other people from different communities – which children acquire at an early age.

> A period abroad, well exploited from the perspective of a sojourner, can develop your own *savoirs*, particularly *savoir s'engager* – critical cultural awareness.

**MOVING** *ON* > > > > > > MOVING *ON* > > > > > > MOVING *ON*

Talk to your primary colleagues who are subject leaders for citizenship, PSHE, religious education amd the humanities to find out about the strategies they use to encourage children to discuss and reflect on values and the kinds of questions they ask.

**FURTHER READING** FURTHER READING **FURTHER READING** FURTHER READING

Alexander, R. (2000) *Culture and pedagogy. International comparisons in primary education*. Oxford: Blackwell Publishing.

Byram, M. and Doyé, P. (1999) Intercultural competence and foreign language learning in the primary school. In Driscoll, P. and Frost, D. (eds) *The teaching of modern foreign languages in the primary school.* London: Routledge.

Council for Subject Associations (CfSA) (2008) *Citizenship – Primary Subjects* magazine, Issue 1.

Datta, M. and Pomphrey, C. (2004) *A world of languages. Developing children's love of languages.* Young Pathfinder 10. London: CILT.

Gregory, A. with Hicks, S. and Comfort, T. (2003) Citizenship and modern foreign languages in the primary school in Brown, K. and Brown. M. (eds).

Jones, B. (1995) *Exploring otherness*. London: CILT.

Newman, E., Taylor, A., Whitehead, J. and Planel, C. (2004) You can't do it like that – it's just wrong! Impressions of French and English trainee primary teachers on exchange placement in primary schools abroad: the value of experiencing the difference. *European Journal of Teacher Education* 27:3, December 2004.

QCA (2007) *The global dimension in action. A curriculum planning guide for schools*. London: QCA. Order from www.qca.org.uk/orderline. Ref: QCA/07/3410.

## Useful websites

www.britishcouncil.org/etwinning.htm – The British Council provides support for schools wishing to become an e-twin with a school in another country.

www.britishcouncil.org/languageassistants.htm – The British Council also provides information on finding a native speaker language assistant.

www.britishcouncil.org/comenius-assistants.htm – provides information about Comenius assistants.

# 7
# Continuity and progression, transfer and transition

## By the end of this chapter you will have:

- considered the issues of continuity and progression as set out in the Key Stage 2 Framework for Languages;
- reflected on medium- and long-term planning;
- reflected on the role of Knowledge about Language and explicit grammar teaching;
- considered how Language Learning Strategies help learners make progress;
- considered recording and reporting and some tools to help the transfer of information;
- appreciated the necessity for liaison between primary and secondary teachers;
- become aware of the new secondary languages curriculum;
- become aware of research-based views on progression in language learning.

This chapter addresses the following Professional Standards for QTS:
**Q2, Q11, Q12, Q14**

This chapter first considers some of the issues linked to continuity and progression, and then reflects on aspects of progression and assessment at key transition points, especially that between the primary and secondary sectors.

Progression in language learning is dependent on a range of variables (Johnstone, 2003). Simply starting earlier, even in Year 3 or below, does not guarantee that children will benefit. Continuity and progression are vital, as Mitchell, Martin and Grenfell acknowledge:

> *The investment of more hours, through an earlier start. has at least the potential to raise general levels of achievement, provided the issues of continuity and progression are properly addressed.*
>
> (1992, p4)

The expectation is that the majority of children, after a four-year programme of language learning in Key Stage 2, will become confident users of the new language. What, according to the Framework, does this actually entail? What kinds of things are they expected to be able to do?

**PRACTICAL TASK** PRACTICAL TASK **PRACTICAL TASK** PRACTICAL TASK **PRACTICAL TASK**

### Starter activity

(You will need your Key Stage 2 Framework.)

(This physical group activity requires some preparation before the session.)

Depending on the size of your group, word process in large font several of the descriptions of the

Learning objectives relating to Oracy, Literacy and Intercultural Understanding*, one statement per coloured A4 sheet. Omit the reference letters and numbers (i.e. O3.4 or L4.2). Where possible, the background colours of each sheet should match the colour coding in the Key Stage 2 Framework for the appropriate year group, so, for example, a single learning objective from Year 3 should be on red paper. Shuffle these and distribute them at random, one coloured sheet per trainee. Ask the trainees to do the following.

- Read your statement.

- Decide which strand (Oracy, Literacy or Intercultural Understanding) your statement corresponds to.

- Decide which National Curriculum year group the learning objectives in your strand relate to.

- Find other trainees with objectives from your strand. (All the Oracy people gather together, for example).

- When you have chosen the order which you think relates to progression, place yourselves in order per strand, Year 3 objectives on the left and Year 6 on the right. (Either make a human line with the statements, stick the coloured sheets in a row as a display or refer to a series of prepared PowerPoint slides.)

- How do children move through the four years of language learning at Key Stage 2?

*If you wish, you may consider each of the strands as separate activities, building up a sequence for Oracy, then for Literacy and finally for Intercultural Understanding on different occasions.*

You may spot the use of key words such as *simple* as in O3.1 *Listen and respond to simple rhymes, stories and songs*, or *familiar* as in L3.1 *Recognise some familiar words in written form*. What else do you notice as the later objectives are reached?

Now let us continue by turning to the Framework itself and discovering where in it we can find information about continuity and progression.

## REFLECTIVE TASK
REFLECTIVE TASK

(You need your Key Stage 2 Framework.)

Look through all three parts of the Framework carefully.

- Note down which sections you need to refer to in order to find out about progression.

- Read each of the sections you find and make notes on how progression is described.

- Bring your notes and your Framework to the session on continuity and progression. Be prepared to discuss your findings.

As we saw in Chapter 3, each year group in Part 1 starts with an A4 *Expectations and Outcomes* page which contains all the objectives (Oracy, Literacy and Intercultural Understanding) in a particular year. This is followed by the *At a Glance* pages for the particular year with a summary of all the learning objectives for all five strands. Thirdly, a double-page spread lists the learning objectives for the year, together with the learning opportunities and links to KAL and LLS. Fourthly, there are the teaching activities for each year group.

Part 1. section 7: *Progression by strand* on pages 67–90 takes the four *Expectations and Outcomes* pages for each year group, and regroups exactly the same text, but this time by strand, so all the Oracy expectations and outcomes – for example, are listed on one A4 side, entitled Oracy – an overview (page 67). There are also Literacy (page 71), and Intercultural Understanding overviews (page 75). Again, the expectations are on the left-hand side of the page, and in the right-hand column, the corresponding outcomes. In addition, the cross-cutting strands of KAL and LLS are summarised.

Each overview page is followed by all the learning objectives for a strand listed sequentially, so, for example, you find all the Oracy objectives for Years 3–6 from O3.1 through to O6.4 on pages 68–69. Again, exactly the same text as is found on the yearly *At a Glance* pages, is regrouped by strand, including the examples, but set out in two columns.

This format is intended to support teachers in monitoring progression across years within each strand, either Oracy, Literacy or Intercultural Understanding. If you are planning for a mixed-age class, these pages are of particular relevance.

There is further guidance in Part 2:4 *Moving on: Using the Framework to ensure progression and continuity.* Pages 45–59 offer classroom stories in the form of spotlights to exemplify what progression in the strands might look like in practice.

Part 3:5 *Progression leaps and bounds* offers an explanation of what is meant by progression in the Key Stage 2 Framework, with substantial advice on planning.

# Planning for progression

The Framework assumes that language learning will be included in the normal planning cycle of the school, building on effective primary practice. Those of you aspiring to be Primary Languages Co-ordinators will need to support your primary colleagues by helping them plan, or indeed planning on their behalf, for continuity and progression via medium- and long-term plans. Part 3 of the Key Stage 2 Framework provides guidance on how to tackle these tasks.

We have already considered short-term planning, including individual lesson plans and segments of lessons (see Chapters 4 and 5). Medium-term plans indicate what will be covered over a series of lessons, usually about half a term's work or five to six weeks. Long-term plans cover what is to be taught over the course of the year, so we can track children's progress. So, for example, the new QCA schemes of work for Key Stage 2 Languages provide an overview for units 1–12, and 13–24. These schemes of work, although they cross-refer within the units to other curriculum areas, are focused on teaching and learning Primary Languages. However, when you consider documentation available to you in schools, you will often find that long-term planning covers all subjects in a particular year group and forms part of a school's overall curriculum plans.

Turn to Part 3, pages 66–67 of the Key Stage 2 Framework where you will find a medium-term plan and a weekly plan based on a cross-curricular theme on planets. If possible, try to access the resources mentioned in the unit, or find similar materials.

---

**PRACTICAL TASK** PRACTICAL TASK **PRACTICAL TASK** PRACTICAL TASK **PRACTICAL TASK**

To bring this task alive, visit www.primarylanguages.org.uk and type the word planets into the search box.

• View the clips in order and note what the teacher and children are doing in each clip.

---

**REFLECTIVE TASK**
REFLECTIVE TASK

(You need your Key Stage 2 Framework.)

Read thoroughly the double-page spreads on pages 67 and 68 which describe work with the Year 5 class on planets, marking what you have observed on the clips.

- How does the teacher find ways to meet all learners' needs, including supporting those who require it and extending others?

- How does she ensure that all children will make progress at their own level?

- Trace progression through the medium-term plan and across the weekly plan.

- View the extracts on www.primarylanguages.org.uk again, with the plans alongside you, so you can link theory with practice.

Part 3 of the Framework provides other examples of long- and medium-term plans. In order to see how a medium-term plan might fit into a longer overview, try the following tasks. If you open the double-page spread entitled Year 3 Long-term overview (Part 3, section 2, page 11) you will find the different curriculum areas listed across the page. Below them, in columns, are various themes. Each column or strand suggests overall themes for six units of work, each one lasting about half a term. So the first overall theme for the first half of the autumn term is *Our community* with suggestions for each curriculum area.

**PRACTICAL TASK** PRACTICAL TASK PRACTICAL TASK PRACTICAL TASK PRACTICAL TASK

(You need your Key Stage 2 Framework, Part 3.)

Everyone in the group should start with Part 3:2, page 11 Year 3 Long-term Overview.

- Familiarise yourself with the main themes across the year in a range of subjects.

- How does the Primary Languages (MFL) theme relate to other curriculum subjects?

- Discuss your impressions.

Once you have a feel for the long-term overview, and how the languages elements fit in with other curriculum subjects such as the humanities, science, design technology, art, music, ICT, PSHE and citizenship, look more closely at the Units of work relating just to Primary Languages on page 9.

**PRACTICAL TASK** PRACTICAL TASK PRACTICAL TASK PRACTICAL TASK PRACTICAL TASK

(You need your Key Stage 2 Framework, Part 3.)

Turn to Part 3:2, page 9 Year 3 Examples of units of work.

- Working in pairs, start by considering the first column for the first half of the autumn term.

- Note down what children might learn in the first six weeks using the headings in the column to help you.

- In your main language, make a brief list of vocabulary and structures you might need to teach linked to the proposed themes.

(If you are short of time, one pair could consider language diversity, a second location of country, a third greetings and a fourth suitable classroom commands for Year 3.)

**PRACTICAL TASK** PRACTICAL TASK PRACTICAL TASK PRACTICAL TASK PRACTICAL TASK

(You need your Key Stage 2 Framework.)

Look at the suggestions for the second half term of the autumn term: *Where in the world?*

- Plan what the first topic – climate/weather – might look like in outline. (Don't forget what you are building on from your first half term suggestions.)
- What would you have to revise?
- What would children be learning which is new?
- Which learning objectives from Year 3 might you be addressing?
- What activities might you plan with the children?
- Feedback your suggestions to the group.

Having considered your own outline medium-term plans, compare the ideas in your group with those in Part 3:2, page 15.

As you can see, individual lessons fit into units of work, and units of work fit into medium- and long-term plans. Use these three sheets to help you understand how this works in practice.

**REFLECTIVE TASK**

Children's language learning should be continuous as they move from year group to year group.

Whole school planning should ensure continuity across successive years of teaching and learning. If your school introduces languages before Key Stage 2, or if it receives children with previous experience of language learning into Key Stage 2, this must be taken account of. As we saw in Chapter 5 on planning, it is vital to build on children's existing knowledge and understanding.

# Helping children progress: Knowledge about Language

As we know from our study of the Key Stage 2 Framework, one of the two transversal strands is Knowledge about Language (KAL). There has been substantial debate about the role of knowledge about language and grammar teaching within languages programmes, and whether children learning languages in school settings should acquire some explicit understandings and knowledge of the nature of language. At the height of the communicative language teaching period, proponents of language competence programmes, which were based on progression in the new language, tended to emphasise use of the target language and the promotion of meaning-oriented target language use. Such teachers were reluctant to incorporate a language awareness or knowledge about language dimension, on the grounds that to do so would shift attention away from maximum target language use and lead to too much discussion in English. However, findings from the early years of the Scottish MLPS initiative (Low et al., 1993, 1995; Low, 1999) together with other European research (Edelenbos and Johnstone, 1996; Blondin et al., 1998) demonstrate the importance of an understanding of L1 and of language *per se* in the development of foreign language competence. Prior to the creation of the Key Stage 2 Framework, Martin (2000b) had already suggested that a future Primary Languages curriculum might encompass knowledge about language.

Indeed, recent years have seen a general return to explicit grammar teaching in many language learning classrooms, or at least advocacy of knowledge about language in various guises within National Curriculum documents and accompanying Frameworks. Currently we have limited evidence about the impact of KAL-related activities in Primary Languages class-rooms, although in a similar manner to the learner strategy research we shall mention in the next section, we do have some studies of British Key Stage 3 languages classrooms in relation to Knowledge about Language (Mitchell, et al., 1994) and Progression (Mitchell and Dickson, 1997).

In the former project, which investigated the teaching of English and foreign languages in Year 9 in three case study schools, language as system (syntax and lexis), at sentence level or below, received the most consistent attention by the modern languages teachers. In contrast, English teachers worked at text level, discussing features of whole texts rather than referring to details at sentence level. Significantly, children in the English and FL class-rooms seemed to receive largely *unrelated* messages in Knowledge about Language. Mitchell et al. (1994) conclude:

> *While many effective KAL episodes were seen, they did not add up to a developmentally coherent curriculum strand.*
>
> (1994, p19)

In this respect, primary teachers of languages have a real opportunity to make connections between English, literacy and languages work and to do so in a less fragmented and episodic way than appeared to be occurring in the study of secondary classrooms.

Mitchell (2003), in her analysis of progression in earlier versions of the MFL National Curriculum, recommends that any languages curriculum should incorporate a language-specific grammar spine. Alongside rote learned expressions with immediate communicative value, learners need to be pushed to encounter and manipulate new grammar patterns with a wider range of verb vocabulary and to use them creatively to make meaning.

By interacting with the new language children can explore how language works. They can use their prior knowledge of their first language to recognise similarities and differences in the new language. The Key Stage 2 Framework states:

> *When children learn a new language they reinterpret and consolidate the knowledge and understanding that they gained in learning their first language(s). They develop insights into the nature of language and its social and cultural significance.*
>
> (DfES, 2005, Part 2:4, p55)

Mitchell (2003) argues that there is significant international research evidence that a **focus on form** within an overall communicative approach is needed to maximise learners' developing control of the foreign language.

> *We must ensure that most learners are making meaningful progress with mastery and the use of the target language system. Although the precise relationship*

between the processing of L2 input (listening and reading), the generation of output (speaking and writing), and the development of the internal target language system is unclear, the existence of such a relationship is undisputed.

(2003, p22) [my emphasis]

REFLECTIVE TASK

## REFLECTIVE TASK

Young language learners need to acquire an **explicit understanding** of the grammatical structures of the new language, particularly of verbs, and of the third person alongside first and second person forms.

In the words of the Key Stage 2 Framework:

*Teachers should encourage children to make explicit comparisons between the new language and English, and to analyse similarities and differences.*

(DfES, 2005, Part 2:4, p55)

Johnstone (1994) proposes introducing knowledge of grammar early on in a child's experience of learning the foreign language, but in a *carefully phased* manner, which encompasses both L1 and the FL. He goes on to suggest the following sequence for the development of grammatical knowledge. [My emphasis]

1. **Recognition** of grammar in **L1 texts**, both spoken and written *(nouns, verbs, adjectives, pronouns, connectives).*
2. **Recognition** of the same in **FL texts**.
3. Recognition of key **grammatical differences** between **L1 and the FL.**
4. The ability to **state** simple rules and to use this knowledge for **comprehension** *(listening and reading).*
5. The ability to **use** these rules, in order to monitor and regulate **spoken** and **written output**.

Johnstone draws attention to holistic approaches to teaching and learning, which involve both the right and left sides of the brain. When the whole brain is engaged, with the two different hemispheres working in unison, some researchers suggest that learners can assimilate higher levels of vocabulary and structure than if only one side of the brain were involved. Songs, rhymes, actions, bright visuals, interactive activities, games and colour coding to highlight patterns can be easily applied in primary school.

With these points from research in mind, reconsider the KAL strands of the Key Stage 2 Framework.

## PRACTICAL TASK PRACTICAL TASK PRACTICAL TASK PRACTICAL TASK PRACTICAL TASK

(You need your Key Stage 2 Framework.)

Turn to Part 1, section 7, pages 78–83 (KAL) and Part 2, section 4, page 55.

- How does the KAL Overview for Years 3–6 fit the insights from research?
- Consider the summary objectives.
- To what extent do the KAL suggestions mirror the findings from research?

- Audit whether you are providing children with opportunities to develop their KAL understanding in some of the ways suggested.

# Teaching grammar in the primary phase: some practical suggestions

**PRACTICAL TASK** PRACTICAL TASK PRACTICAL TASK PRACTICAL TASK PRACTICAL TASK

You will need access to the internet.

(For the feedback session, your tutor might like to download the videos to support discussion.)

Go to www.primarylanguages.org.uk. Go to the Key Stage 2 Framework, and Knowledge about Language. You will find that there are at least 16 examples of teachers and children working on KAL.

- Choose a different example each and be prepared to discuss the approaches and ideas collaboratively.
- How do the practical examples you have viewed link with the theoretical picture we have been discussing above?
- Discuss your findings. (Have you observed teachers in your placement schools using similar techniques to raise children's awareness of knowledge about language?)
- Which particular clip would you like to emulate and why?
- Try out at least one of these suggestions in your next teaching placement.

When reviewing the examples you have seen demonstrated, either for real in the classroom, or virtually on the Primary Languages Training Zone, it may be helpful to consider the guidelines on grammar and KAL in Appendix 3.

Johnstone makes clear that there is evidence that if learners develop a strong command of their first language, this will help them learn the new language. He also states:

> *Pupils will make more rapid progress in the language if the concepts they are dealing with are already to some extent familiar to them. If they have to learn totally new concepts as well as the language that represents these, then progress will be slower.*

> (1994, p61)

Throughout it is vital to build on L1 concepts which children are already familiar with and to-explicitly make links between work in English and literacy and work in the new language by:

- comparing and contrasting, not only with English, but with other languages represented in your classroom;
- making use of the metalanguage available, with which children are familiar from English lessons.
- doing physical actions to help children remember nouns, pronouns, adjectives, verbs, adverbs, connectives, prepositions, etc.

## REFLECTIVE TASK

(You need the QCA schemes of work.)

Consider one of the later units in the language which you intend to teach.

- With a partner make a list of the grammatical elements related to the unit which you think it would be important to begin to teach children.
- What aspects might it be appropriate to prioritise?
- What grammatical areas might children find tricky?
- How could you help them understand and apply the patterns?

# Helping children progress – Language Learning Strategies

A further means of helping children make progress in the new language is to support them in developing their language learning strategies – the second of the cross-cutting strands in the Key Stage 2 Framework. So why have language learning strategies been incorporated into this document?

As we saw in Chapter 3, their inclusion has come about in part owing to the switch in foreign languages pedagogy from teaching to learning, which occurred during the 1990s. Key writers are Nisbet and Shucksmith (1986) who reviewed learning strategies. In fact, learning strategies in general are connected to language learning strategies, since many of the techniques adopted by language learners are common across subjects. For instance, Harris and Grenfell (2004) have indicated some of the commonalities in strategic use between English (L1) and foreign languages (L2).

Learning strategies are to do with what makes a successful language learner. Studies of the 'good language learner' go back some three decades. Naiman et al. (1978) and Stern (1975) sought to identify the tactics adopted by successful language learners to guide their learning. Other researchers, O'Malley and Chamot (1990) claim that L2 acquisition is not just an intuitive, natural process but entails the employment of a number of strategies – cognitive, metacognitive and social/affective.

Cognition is to do with the *direct processing of the language, and* metacognition *with thinking about* these processes. Cognition may include a range of language processes, from techniques for memorising vocabulary to those which infer meaning from text. Metacognition, in contrast, is to do with guiding the learning process itself, and includes strategies for planning, monitoring and evaluating language use, a point taken up by Mitchell, who recommends that language learners should be provided with opportunities to reflect explicitly on learning styles and:

> *develop strategies for planning, reflection, monitoring and evaluation of their own performance*

> (Mitchell, 2003, p22)

This view emphasises what learners themselves can consciously do in order to achieve success. So what does the good language learner do, which poorer language learners fail to do? Rubin, also writing in 1990, encourages us to make clear to learners the kinds of strategies which are helpful in tackling a new language, pointing out:

> *Often poorer learners don't have a clue as to how good learners arrive at their answers and feel that they can never perform as good learners do. By revealing the process, this myth can be exposed.*

(1990, p282)

## REFLECTIVE TASK

Working individually, spend a few moments reflecting on your own language learning experience.

- Note down what you did in order to be a successful language learner.
- How did you go about memorising vocabulary?
- How did you learn grammar rules?
- What did you do when you were listening to a CD or watching a DVD and did not quite understand something?
- How did you work out the meaning of a reading text with unfamiliar language?
- How did you set about writing a text and checking it?
- Share the list of strategies you have identified with others in your group.

Research indicates that successful language learners:

- employ a **range of strategies**;
- have a **wider repertoire** than do less effective learners;
- apply the strategies more **frequently**;
- also **deploy metacognitive** strategies.

The majority of international language learner strategy studies have tended to focus on adults and on the learning of English as an L2. Presently, there is a notable dearth of research related to learner strategies and primary language learners in the UK, although we do have one study relating to Bangladeshi children's strategies for learning to read in UK primary school settings (Walters, 2007). A much earlier study, the evaluation of the Scottish MLPS pilot in the early 1990s (Low et al, 1995), also commented on primary age language learners' awareness of strategies.

What we do have are some emerging findings from researchers working as part of the UKPOLLS (UK Project on Language Learner Strategies) group. In contrast to the adult studies, their work considers secondary MFL students in England. Thus, in the UKPOLLS' studies, the subjects are typically (near) beginner language learners in secondary schools, learning languages such as French, German, Spanish and Italian, rather than English, on account of the British context.

Examples are Erler (2007) on Year 7 learners strategies for reading French, Harris (2007) on a project to implement strategy instruction relating to listening and reading – in other words to explicitly teach learners 'how to listen' and 'how to read' – with 12–13-year-old children in two London schools learning French over a one-year period, and Macaro (2007) on free writing by Year 7 learners of French.

Although the context is not identical to that in the languages classroom in the primary school in England, nonetheless several findings are relevant to us as Primary Languages practitioners. For instance, Macaro's study of Year 7 free writers reports that:

- more effective writers monitored and checked their work during the process of composition;
- Year 7 'free writers' were limited to writing about topics which they were currently studying – this meant that they did not need to retrieve language from their long-term memory;
- the main formulation strategy appeared to be to:
  - recall a set phrase (one of the formulaic, prefabricated phrases we mentioned above in relation to KAL), which approximately matched what they wanted to say;
  - avoid expressing the idea altogether if they could not remember the 'set-phrase'.

## REFLECTIVE TASK

Children did not seem to realise that phrases could be recombined or restructured, and there was little evidence of them attempting to generate their own utterances.

## REFLECTIVE TASK

What implications do these findings have for:

- the demands we make on learners to write 'freely' and 'creatively';
- the incorporation of KAL, dictionary skills and grammar in our teaching?

Strategies require lots of practice and take time to develop. In order for language learners to become creative and write for meaning even at near beginner level, we therefore need to:

- provide plenty of opportunities to be creative with the new language;
- model writing for learners;
- encourage writing 'outside the topic';
- work on dictionary skills.

Macaro (2007) suggests that there should be a considerable increase in free-writing without access to resources, except perhaps a dictionary, encouraging learners to formulate by choosing from the whole range of strategies. This teaching may produce more inaccurate writing in the short term.

## REFLECTIVE TASK

- Do you agree that learner strategies can be taught to young learners or should they apply more to older (secondary school) language learners?
- Are some strategies easier than others?
- Might some skill areas be more suitable for beginner 'strategy instruction' than others?
- What can teachers do to encourage the development of language learning strategies?

# Language Learning Strategies in the Key Stage 2 Framework

In Part 1, section 7 *Progression by strand*, language learning strategies are presented in an overview on page 84. One of the aims of language learning in Key Stage 2 is to:

> *familiarise children with strategies which they can apply to the learning of **any** language.*

The overview continues:

> *Children can be helped to see how they have used language learning strategies in the acquisition of their first language(s), how they are using them in learning the new language and how they might use them in future language learning as well as in more general learning in other areas of the curriculum.*
>
> (DfES, 2005, Part 1:7, p84)

In the light of the research above, you will find Part 1:7, pages 85–90, especially helpful. On these pages the language learning strategies are classified into six broad categories with some examples. The strategies are grouped under the following headings:

- Planning, analysing and evaluating ways of learning;
- Communicating: understanding and being understood;
- Practising language;
- Memorising;
- Applying prior knowledge;
- Dictionary skills.

(You need your Key Stage 2 Framework.)

Turn to Part 1, section 7, pages 84–90. Study carefully the points made below the subheadings.

- Use these as a checklist to help you audit the range of learning strategies you are encouraging children to develop.

Bear in mind the following:

> *To maximise the potential benefits of this process [of strategy use] the Framework helps teachers to make this learning explicit. In the early years of Key Stage 2 they can discuss... how rhymes help [children] remember words and phrases and how the context in which they encounter a word can help them determine its meaning and subsequently recall it. Later in Key Stage 2 children will extend their capabilities to include skills such as using a bilingual dictionary and memorising language. By Year 6 children should have developed a repertoire of techniques...*
>
> (DfES, Part 2:4, p55 [my emphasis])

At the time of going to press, there are ten new sets of activities associated with the theme Language Learning Strategies on the Primary Languages website.

---

**PRACTICAL TASK** PRACTICAL TASK PRACTICAL TASK PRACTICAL TASK PRACTICAL TASK

(You will need access to the internet.)

Go to www.primarylanguages.org.uk. Go to the Key Stage 2 Framework and select the sub-theme LLS.

- View a selection of the video clips in which links are made to language learning strategies.
- Choose one in particular which you feel is especially effective. Present it to your peers.
- Try to incorporate at least one idea from the extract you have chosen in your own practice.

---

As we come to consider the recording and reporting of children's progress, let us revisit the notion of progression by considering the expectations and outcomes as well as the learning objectives, on which we reflected in our starter task.

---

**PRACTICAL TASK** PRACTICAL TASK PRACTICAL TASK PRACTICAL TASK PRACTICAL TASK

(You need your Key Stage 2 Framework.)

Look at the Overview sheets on pages 67, 71 and 75.

- Focusing on both columns, with a highlighter mark the key features in the descriptions for each of the four years.
- Trace the progression in children's learning over the four years. What do you notice?
- How would you summarise features of progression?
- Compare your findings with the suggestions below.

---

You can see that the intention is that children move from the simple to the more complex, from single words to longer sentences, from needing a high level of support to initiating conversations confidently. Taking also into account increased knowledge about language and language learning strategies:

- the amount and complexity of the language which children understand and can use should increase;
- they should understand more about how language and languages work;
- their understanding of their own culture and other people's culture should grow;
- the range and frequency of use of language learning strategies should rise;
- their responses should become more fluent;
- they should be able to reuse language in different contexts and topics;
- they should be more confident in coping with unpredictable language;
- they should be able to deduce meaning more confidently on the basis of grammatical knowledge;
- they should be more independent language learners and users.

(adapted from DfES, 2005, Part 3:5, p65)

Key statements are that *there is not just one way in which children make progress in a language*. And *you should not worry if they develop unevenly or if you see only some of these features at some times...* These comments can be linked with research findings.

# Progression: a research perspective

Johnstone (1994, 33) tells us that learners can be expected to make progress by:

- becoming more fluent, more accurate and more wide ranging in their use of language;

- dealing with increasingly longer and more complex language;
- undertaking tasks with a progressively more demanding cognitive level.

BEFLECTIVE TASK

### REFLECTIVE TASK

But... does progress occur in a regular, systematic way, evenly across all these parameters or does it do so at different rates?

Does progress in one area, for example fluency, for a while mean regress in another, say grammatical control and accuracy?

- Consider your own progress as a language learner as well as that of children with whom you have come in contact.
- What are your views on the above questions?

Progression in language learning is more like 'snakes and ladders' – some aspects go up, others go down (see Mitchell and Myles, 1998).

We can all recall being taught a grammatical rule as part of a language lesson and perhaps being able to manipulate the particular structure in practice exercises reasonably accurately at the time. However, we also know that when we try to create language more spontaneously, after a lapse of time, the grammar point may appear in our repertoire, but not quite in its correct form. This is because the grammar rule, though consciously taught and learned, was not fully internalised. An explanation for this is that foreign or L2 language learners are said to pass through a series of interim languages, known as **'inter-languages'** as they progress towards greater proficiency.

When we consider spontaneous spoken output, we can see that very often learners use what are termed prefabricated chunks. Examples of formulaic phrases are *Comment tu t'appelles?'* or *Tu as des frères et des sœurs?* or *J'ai dix ans.* These memorised phrases may be quite long and be linked to form strings of phrases. They are often structurally complex and are employed 'whole' and 'off the shelf' as it were, yielding grammatically 'correct' utterances. In contrast, when grammar is used to create new utterances, the phrases are typically shorter, even one or two words only, and incorporate inter-language features. The way in which beginner learners gradually 'unpack' these memorised phrases over time can be shown by a research study of Key Stage 3 learners of French (Mitchell and Dickson, 1997; Mitchell and Martin, 1997). The example below shows how *Comment t'appelles-tu?* was gradually adapted to express *What's the boy called?*

Memorised phrases were used, unaltered and often over extended in meaning.
*Comment t'appelles-tu*? was used when the child wanted to say *What's the boy called?*

Extra words were added to the memorised phrases to clarify meaning.
*Comment t'appelles-tu **le garçon**?*

Choice points and potential breaks within memorised phrases were identified.
*Comment t'appelles le garçon?*

Comment s'appelle le garçon?

Learners sorted out the basic components of French sentences and began to freely combine nouns, pronouns and verbs in grammatical patterns. However, gains made by children in underlying grammatical understanding was regularly accompanied by some loss of surface accuracy, i.e. errors in verb endings temporarily increased. The key role of **verbs** in early language learning was re-emphasised by the vocabulary study.

Memorised phrases have great significance in early language teaching and teachers in this study spent a good deal of lesson time providing opportunities for learners to practise them in pair and group work. Great emphasis was placed on spoken French in line with communicative methodology but little formal grammar teaching occurred. Teachers did do consciousness-raising activities, i.e. they drew attention to features such as gender or compared spoken and written forms. These tactics seemed to have immediate usefulness in helping children informally to get started on the analysis of the memorised phrases.

Continuity, progression and eventually some form of record keeping and/or assessment feed into information which we transfer at various transition points, and particularly at the major transition between primary and secondary school.

Pollard reminds us that *informal, but principled, professional conversation between past and future teachers at times of transition and transfer is extremely valuable in bringing documentary information to life* (2005, p348).

# Liaising with associated secondary schools and across primary and secondary clusters

Primary and secondary teachers co-operating and working together is clearly the most important feature in the future success of Primary Languages. The implications of the statement that secondary and primary schools must communicate are far reaching. They highlight the fact that the specific working relationship between Key Stage 2 and Key Stage 3 languages teachers is vital for a successful transition. For languages work in primary school to have a real impact, secondary teachers must have truly accepted what the children they receive in Year 7 know, understand and can do. If they know what the children have been studying they can continue to build on that learning and allow them to make real progress. Despite the fact that progression in learning is important in considering the concept of transition to secondary school, secondary schools often ignore or dismiss prior learning. There are a number of assumptions that are made on both sides which can be addressed by working together.

In the Framework for Languages, Part 2, section 5 it states that for effective continuity and progression between Year 6 children in primary as they transfer to Year 7 in secondary school, the teachers in the two phases need to communicate, which is the key to effective transition and transfer. The Key Stage 2 Framework states:

> *It will become increasingly important for teachers of secondary pupils to know what children have learnt, understood and achieved during Key Stage 2 if they are properly to provide for progression and continuity in language learning.*
>
> (DfES, 2005, Part 2, p66)

REFLECTIVE TASK

**REFLECTIVE TASK**

- Discuss the kinds of assessment information it would be helpful to agree upon between Key Stage 2 and Key Stage 3 in order to ease the transition.
- What form might this information take?
- Share your findings with the rest of your group.
- Compare your suggestions with those in the Key Stage 2 Framework, Part 2, p67.

Cross-phase clusters will need to agree on the following issues:

- what kind of information about Key Stage 2 teaching is most useful for Key Stage 3 staff;
- what kind of information about Key Stage 3 teaching is most useful for Key Stage 2 staff;
- what kind of child records are most helpful to pass on from partner primaries to the teachers of children in Year 7;
- what opportunities Year 6 children might have to meet Year 7 teachers before transferring;
- what opportunities there are for cross-phase curriculum developments.

# Recording and reporting in Primary Languages

Currently, although many teachers carry out informal, continuous assessment as part of their teaching, assessment, recording and reporting are rather weak areas of Primary Languages and as yet, underdeveloped (Muijs et al., 2005). Nonetheless, you will need to make decisions about what to record and how to record it.

The Key Stage 2 Framework therefore advises:

> *As language learning is extended to progress over four years from Years 3–6, it will be important for schools to build in a more systematic programme of assessment so that children's progress can be properly monitored over the four years. Assessment data can then be passed on through the school to each new teacher and then to the secondary school to ensure progression and continuity.*
>
> (DCSF, 2007, Part 3:7, p111)

The first question, about what needs to be recorded, has to do with the purpose of the recording and assessment. Records of attainment must be kept for each child in each National Curriculum subject. At the time of writing, languages are not yet statutory, but are likely to become so from 2010/11 in response to the Languages Review (Dearing and King, 2007).

Records can be used to:

- help inform the teacher as to how to guide the next steps in teaching and learning;
- show what children know, understand and can do, and the progress that they have made;
- enable children to see the progress they are making;
- provide information for setting targets at all levels – individual, group and cohort;
- inform discussions with parents, and end-of-year reports;

- provide accurate information about a child's attainment, progress and learning needs which can be passed on to the next teacher or school;
- inform subject co-ordinators of any changes required to medium-term plans and schemes of work.

# Assessment of learning: summative assessment

In Chapter 5 on planning, we briefly considered formative assessment and AfL, which looks forward to what is to be achieved and is prospective. This contrasts with Assessment of learning (AoL), which attempts to sum up a child's attainment in a given area of the curriculum. Summative assessment is retrospective: it looks back on what the child has achieved.

The Key Stage 2 Framework sets out expectations for what most children should be able to do by the end of each year. We have already referred to these in the earlier section on progression (see page 103). In Part 3, section 7 there is guidance on both types of assessment.

### Sources of assessment evidence

Assessing learning is about collecting evidence and making judgments about what children have been learning. The evidence can be based on:

- what learners say;
- what learners do;
- what learners produce;
- what learners feel or think.

# Transfer and transition

Recording has a key role to play in the effective transfer of information when children move from one school to another and particularly between Key Stage 2 and Key Stage 3, and from one class to another within the same school.

In order that the next teacher or school can extend children's present attainment, build on their strengths and address any areas for development, key pieces of information from the present teacher's knowledge must be passed on in a manageable way.

The Key Stage 2 Framework advises:

> *If individual pupil records are to be transferred they need to be informative, reliable and manageable. They should not be an excessive burden for primary teachers to compile nor constitute an unrealistic mass of information for secondary teachers to assimilate. They should add a language dimension to the pupil data already transferred to receiving secondary schools and indicate what a pupil knows, understands and can do in the language(s) learnt.*
>
> (DfES, 2005, Part 2, p67)

# Language learning portfolios

In the section in Part 3:7, page 113 there is a description of the use of the child portfolios as part of effective practice in assessing languages. A series of suggestions indicate how to involve children in their own learning, progress and assessment.

**PRACTICAL TASK** PRACTICAL TASK **PRACTICAL TASK** PRACTICAL TASK **PRACTICAL TASK**

Do any of your placement schools use their own portfolio, an LA or cluster document, or the European Language Portfolio (ELP), in order to pass on records to secondary schools? Discuss what you have experienced.

- How were the portfolios or similar documents being used?
- Do you think they are effective?
- What disadvantages and advantages of this kind of recording can you foresee?

## European Language Portfolio

The educational need for formative and self-assessment in Primary Languages is an area where a growing number of assessment initiatives are being reported. Portfolios offer a useful way of keeping evidence of learning. Most of the work in this area centres round versions of the ELP, an initiative of the Council of Europe. This includes the junior version of the ELP, *My Languages Portfolio,* originally published by CILT in 2001. This was revised to take account of the Key Stage 2 Framework for Languages. There is also a revised Teacher's Guide. You or the children can download the portfolio at www.nacell.org. uk/resources/resources.htm and complete sections electronically. Alternatively hard copies can be purchased.

The Portfolio belongs to the children. Used under the teacher's guidance, it gives children ownership of their learning and a sense of pride in what they can do. The Portfolio promotes a reflective approach to language learning as well as being a tool for assessing and recording. You and the children can see their progress at a glance.

An open-ended record of linguistic achievement, the Portfolio:

- shows what children know, understand and can do and the progress they have made;
- enables children to see the progress they are making;
- provides information about a child's progress, which can be passed on to the next teacher or school.

It is non-statutory: you do not have to use it. You might like to adapt some of the ideas in it – especially the *can-do* statements.

The Portfolio has three sections.

- My language biography (pages 3–15).
- My dossier (page 17).
- My language passport (pages 21–33).

**My language biography** is an ever changing part of the Portfolio which children can update regularly. They do this by colouring in *can-do* statements and completing them as they progress, building up a personalised learning diary. The revised version also enables them to indicate achievements in intercultural understanding and language learning strategies.

**My dossier** is for the collection of children's own work. Children are free to add to and remove pieces of work as they move through the school. You might encourage them to include digital photographs of themselves listening to a story, singing a song, doing a

PowerPoint presentation, sharing their work in an assembly, or even audio or video files – the possibilities are endless.

The final part, **My language passport**:

- summarises language learning experiences and levels reached;
- uses self-assessment check lists, linked to the **Languages Ladder** (see below);
- covers contacts and intercultural experiences and languages learned both at home and in school.

The first stage of the Languages Ladder Breakthrough (divided into three grades), is the one we are concerned with in the primary phase. (Examples of further stages and grades are also provided for comparison.)

---

**PRACTICAL TASK** PRACTICAL TASK PRACTICAL TASK PRACTICAL TASK PRACTICAL TASK

(You need copies of the Portfolio.)

Your tutor will need to prepare envelopes each containing sets of statements on separate strips. See Appendix 4 on pages 149–151.

- Take the envelope and use the grey strips to spread out the six skills and areas of experience in a row. Use these as column headings. Beneath each of them place up to five statements which match the heading.

- Compare your statements with the ones in the speech bubbles on pages 10–15 of *My Languages Portfolio*.

---

You will find more information about the ELP the Key Stage 2 Framework Part 3, page 114.

# The National Languages Recognition Scheme: the Languages Ladder

The National Languages Strategy states:

> *By age 11 [children] should have the opportunity to reach a recognised level of competence on the Common European Framework and for that achievement to be recognised through a national scheme.*

(DfES, 2002, p15)

A growth area is consequently the development of free-standing proficiency tests referenced to nationally and internationally recognised scales, which form the basis for 'portable' certification in a variety of languages. In the UK, Asset Languages is a major government funded initiative providing proficiency tests in four language skills in a range of languages, mapped to the Languages Ladder developed by the DCSF.

The National Recognition Scheme, the Languages Ladder, is a voluntary system which enables children and teachers to assess achievement using a series of *can-do* statements in the skills of listening, speaking, reading and writing. In fact, the Languages Ladder is intended for learners of all ages.

### Key features of the Languages Ladder
- Designed to endorse the learner's achievement.

- Based on *can-do* statements.
- Provides assessment opportunities in just one skill in any one language in either listening, speaking, reading or writing.
- Offers possibilities for teacher assessment within each stage.
- Provides voluntary external assessment at the end of each stage.

There is no expectation that learners will be at the same grade in each of the four skills at any one time. Examples of *can-do* statements in Listening are as follows.

- 1: I can understand a few familiar spoken words and phrases.
- 2: I can understand a range of familiar spoken phrases.
- 3: I can understand the main points from a short spoken passage.

---

**PRACTICAL TASK** PRACTICAL TASK PRACTICAL TASK PRACTICAL TASK PRACTICAL TASK

(You will need the Key Stage 2 Framework for Languages.)

Turn to Part 3, p112. Read the section within the box entitled *Expectations for most children*.

- At what grade on the Languages Ladder is it anticipated that most children will be working at the end of four years of language study in the primary school?
- What is the overall achievement of most children in the two strands of Oracy and Literacy in at least one language intended to be?
- Check the actual *can-do* statements from the Languages Ladder descriptors. Do they surprise you? How can you support children to achieve these grades?

---

It is noteworthy that whereas in the past there have been a variety of level descriptors for different skill areas, for instance National Curriculum Attainment Target levels for listening, speaking, reading and writing, differently worded descriptors within the junior version of the European Language Portfolio and again on the Languages Ladder, all these levels have now been aligned to correspond with the Common European Framework, an internationally recognised standard of achievement in languages. This will make assessment much clearer to understand as all formal documents will be similarly worded.

**A note of caution**: The National Curriculum for secondary MFL has hitherto identified progression by level descriptions within the attainment targets (ATs) in the separate skills of listening, speaking, reading and writing, and as we can see, a ladder with graded steps is a useful means of recording progress. However, language learning is a very long process, and the benefits of Primary Languages are not easily measurable. Furthermore, when planning for continuity and progression, we need to be aware that research into language learning has demonstrated that language learning is more complex than the systematic, stepwise ladder metaphor of language development might seem to indicate; rather it is a recursive process with *multiple interconnections and backslidings, and complex trade-offs between advances in accuracy, fluency and complexity* (Mitchell, 2003, p17).

It is important to successfully integrate the development of learners' understanding of the target language systems with learners' developing capability for target language use. Mitchell (2003) makes the point that there is no reason in principle why language learners even at the lowest levels should not be engaging in much longer conversational exchanges than currently recommended in National Curriculum level descriptors. Indeed, she states that there is no reason why language learners should not be referring to past, present and future, even as beginning language learners.

## 7–14 continuum

Finally, in order to get a longer-term view of continuity and progression, Primary Languages Co-ordinators need to know about the early Key Stage 3 curriculum and what children will be progressed towards.

It is important for there to be a two-way flow of information and for some secondary teachers, especially those with responsibility for liaison work with primaries, to know first hand what is happening in the primary phase. This can occur through reciprocal visits and observations, not just of languages lessons, but of the whole primary curriculum, in order to genuinely inform practice after transition. Martin (2000), in the review of national and international research into school-based language learning conducted on behalf of QCA, stated quite clearly the importance of regarding the Key Stage 2/Key Stage 3 curriculum as a coherent whole, rather than two separate entities. Since then there have been moves towards a new paradigm for language learning in which 7–14 is viewed as a continuum as described by Dr Lid King, in many presentations. See diagram in Appendix 5 on page 153.

# The new secondary curriculum for languages

More recently still, the QCA has reconceptualised the secondary curriculum to make it broader and more relevant, including a new secondary curriculum for languages. This means that Primary Languages Co-ordinators in particular should keep an eye on changes taking place in secondary schools as from September 2008. More information about the new curriculum for languages can be found at www.all-nsc.org.uk. The new programmes of study for languages at Key Stage 3 can be viewed or downloaded at curriculum.qca.org.uk. The new secondary curriculum fits much more closely with the pedagogy and teaching approaches for languages in the primary school. The curriculum is more flexible and intended to encourage teachers to plan in terms of developing children's language skills, rather than coverage of topics, with an emphasis on engaging and inspiring learners. A key statement is that:

> The introduction, from 2010, of the entitlement for every child to learn a foreign language at key stage 2 implies a fundamental change in the attitudes and expectations of learners as they start key stage 3.
>
> (QCA)

In connection with our theme of progression, we find that in the new secondary curriculum:

- teaching should focus on developing children's linguistic ability and confidence, increasing the range and complexity of language they are able to use and challenging them to apply their knowledge in different situations;
- the revised programme of study encourages teachers to root language learning firmly in the cultural context of the target language;
- teachers should provide plenty of opportunities for children to use their linguistic knowledge imaginatively in different contexts;
- there is greater flexibility over the languages which schools may teach – which may affect cluster decisions about language choice in the primary phase.

The new secondary languages curriculum now builds more smoothly and closely on the foundation being laid in primary school. At secondary level there are key concepts and processes which are clearly linked with the preceding Key Stage 2 Framework for Languages:

- **Key concepts for languages**:
  - Linguistic competence;
  - Knowledge about language;
  - Creativity;
  - Intercultural understanding.

- **Key processes for languages**:
  - Developing language-learning strategies;
  - Developing language skills.

Web-based support, guidance materials and case studies are available at: curriculum.qca. org.uk and all-languages.org.uk.

## A SUMMARY OF **KEY POINTS**

The following are central to language learning.

> *Interaction* is an important element, particularly opportunities to reuse and restructure memorised expressions, grammar patterns, and vocabulary, and apply them in new contexts. We can provide learners with opportunities to do this through increased provision of pair and group work.

> *Scaffolding* is a significant indicator of progression, as learners move from great dependence on their interlocutor to showing increasing independence and initiative.

> *Creativity* and *risk taking* should be encouraged even though accuracy appears to be threatened and should be clearly rewarded in assessment systems.

> *Explicit grammar* is of considerable importance both in planned production (speaking and writing) and in planned and spontaneous comprehension (listening and reading).

> When we teach language learning strategies to children we need to make our own knowledge about how to learn a language successfully, explicit.

**MOVING** *ON* > > > **> > >** MOVING *ON* > > > **> > >** MOVING *ON*

Continuity and progression, transfer and transition continue to be some of the most challenging aspects of Primary Languages initiatives. Investigate actual progression and transition practices in feeder primary and receiving secondary schools that you know, and discuss with your mentor teachers in placement schools how they are dealing with these issues.

**FURTHER READING** FURTHER READING **FURTHER READING** FURTHER READING

Bevis, R. and Gregory, G. (2006) Mind *the gap! Improving transition between Key Stage 2 and Key Stage 3*. Young Pathfinder 13. London: CILT.

Cheater, C. and Farren, A. (2001) *The literacy link*. Young Pathfinder 9. London: CILT.

Jones, J. and Coffey, S. (2006) Teaching approaches – differentiation, motivation and learning across the curriculum, in Jones, J. and Coffey, S. (2006) *Modern foreign languages 5–11*. London: David Fulton Publishers.

Jones, J. and Coffey, S. (2006) Learner strategies and preferences – overcoming the tricky bits, in Jones, J. and Coffey, S. (2006) *Modern foreign languages 5-11*. London: David Fulton Publishers.

Mitchell, R. (2003) Rethinking the concept of progression in the National Curriculum for Modern Foreign Languages: a research perspective. *Language Learning Journal* 27, 15–23.

QCA (2007) Progression in early language learning. Appendix 1. Teacher's Guide (pp 26–27).

## Useful websites

www.primarylanguages.org.uk/ – has examples related to themes in this chapter

www.cilt.org.uk/faqs/sen.htm – The National Centre for Languages website for teachers includes information sheets and discussion boards

www.hilarymccoll.co.uk – website created by a teacher who has extensive experience teaching children with special needs

www.nacell.org.uk/ – provides the junior version of the European Language Portfolio

www.dcsf.gov.uk/languages/DSP_languagesladder.cfm – gives details of the Languages Ladder

www.assetlanguages.org.uk – links you to the Asset Languages site

# 8

# Implementing the languages entitlement: decisions for Primary Languages Co-ordinators

By the end of this chapter you will have:

- understood more about what being an effective Primary Languages Co-ordinator entails;
- prepared to carry out a languages audit in your school;
- become aware of key decisions a Primary Languages Co-ordinator may need to make in order to implement the Key Stage 2 entitlement;
- appreciated the need to work in partnership with both primary and secondary colleagues;
- found out how to create a languages policy for your school;
- gained some understanding of what makes successful clusters and networks;
- recognised the qualities of an effective subject leader/Primary Languages Co-ordinator.

This chapter addresses the following Professional Standards for QTS:
Q6, Q7, Q8, Q14, Q15, Q20, Q22

Many of you working with this book are aspiring to become future Primary Languages Co-ordinators. As such, you will be taking on a leadership role related to the decision making and support for Primary Languages required in your school and, possibly, in the surrounding area.

Even as a newly qualified teacher with a languages specialism, you are likely to find yourself asked to contribute to management decisions, as you may be the person in the school best informed about Primary Languages.

## REFLECTIVE TASK

The entitlement as set out in the National Languages Strategy (DfES, 2002, p15) implies that the first cohort of children to have experienced four years of Primary Languages provision will start in secondary school as Year 7 students in September 2010. What are the implications for co-ordinators?

## Building bridges

Key issues for the Primary Languages Co-ordinator are:

- building bridges internally, within your own school;
- building bridges externally, outside your school with other primary and secondary schools.

# Building bridges within your school

Let's start with your role in your new school.

REFLECTIVE TASK
## REFLECTIVE TASK

### Initial fact finding

Imagine you are in your first teaching post.

- Whom within in your new school might it be important to talk to about Primary Languages?
- Why?
- Discuss what **key questions** you might want to ask to find out about existing languages provision in the school.

## Initial fact finding

In your discussions with your fellow trainees and your tutor you may have come up with similar suggestions to the following, in order to find out the state of Primary Languages provision in your current school. These questions are most suited to be put to the head teacher or someone in the senior management team with an overview of provision. If you are in an interview for a future teaching appointment and the school already has a Primary Languages Co-ordinator, they would be suitable questions to ask in order to ascertain the current situation for languages in your prospective school. (Later, as a Primary Languages Co-ordinator, you may well find yourself answering similar questions.)

- Is any language teaching happening at the moment?
- If yes, what is the tradition of Primary Languages teaching in the school? How many years has the school been teaching Primary Languages and what is the pattern of provision?
- What languages other than English are currently being taught? Which year groups are being taught? Is this in curriculum time or in an extended activity such as a club? How many children are taking part?
- Who does the teaching? Are teaching assistants or foreign language assistants involved in delivering languages as well?
- Are Key Stage 1 children being taught a Primary Language too?
- If no languages teaching is happening, has there been any teaching in the past?
- If it has been discontinued, why was this?
- What is the attitude of staff to Primary Languages?

This last question, if posed to the head teacher, may provide only a partial picture of teachers' views. So having ascertained the facts about languages provision in the school, your next step will possibly be to conduct a short languages audit. This is one way of discovering the wishes of fellow teachers and finding out individual teachers' views and needs.

REFLECTIVE TASK
## REFLECTIVE TASK

### A languages audit – questions for individuals

Imagine you are now preparing to carry out a languages audit.

- Jot down about half a dozen questions you would ask colleagues in order to discover their languages experiences, strengths, needs and attitudes.
- Compare your suggestions with those of your fellow trainees and draw up a list.

One way to obtain a picture of what is happening is to devise a short questionnaire, on one side of A4 paper, and request your head teacher's permission to present it and have it completed in a staff meeting. Doing so means that hopefully you will not have to chase people up, since the questionnaire will be done on the spot, saving everyone time. The following example may be useful – adjust the questions and spacing to suit. As you will be aiming eventually for a whole school policy with everyone involved to some extent, consult assistants as well as teachers.

---

**Languages audit**

*Please answer these questions about your experience of learning and teaching languages.*

What knowledge/experience of languages do you have?

What qualifications do you have in languages?

Would you be interested in developing your language skills?

What support and resources would help?

If you were provided with resources, training and support, would you be prepared to teach a language to your own class?

Which language or languages do you think would most benefit the children in our school?

What would be the benefits to you in terms of professional development?

What other comments would you like to make?

---

**REFLECTIVE TASK**

Check whether Primary Languages are incorporated as a defined priority in the School Development Plan. If they are not, request that they might be.

# Building bridges outside your school

Once you have some idea of the language learning context in your school and what people's prior experiences, views, strengths and needs are, you have to find ways of building on what you have by working with other colleagues outside your school.

**Outside your school**, to a greater or lesser extent, depending on local factors such as LA policies, you are likely to find:

- a variety of provision, aims, teaching approaches and priorities;
- different approaches to continuity and progression;
- issues for everyone related to time – for meeting, for planning, for preparing resources, for delivering lessons, for assessing children;
- perhaps some funding constraints, although this will vary.

For many years, the two age ranges 5–11, and 11–16/18 were viewed as separate entities with few links between them, whereas as we saw in Chapter 7, we are now experiencing a shift towards a new paradigm for 7–14.

## Let's talk! Communication and dialogue are essential for successful Primary Languages programmes

Firstly, do not be tempted to go it alone. Find out who the other Primary Languages Co-ordinators are in neighbouring primary schools, especially those which feed into similar secondary schools to yours. Make sure you have **horizontal liaison** – that **primary schools in your cluster** or locality are talking to each other about languages provision. The National Languages Strategy recommends that all primary schools appoint someone to act as Primary Languages Co-ordinator, so there should be someone with whom you can get in touch.

Primary ⟷ Primary

After a cluster of primaries have got to know each other and shared ideas and concerns, ensure that you have **vertical liaison**:

Secondary

Primary

You should find that increasing numbers of secondary languages departments have allocated the task of liaison with primary schools to one of their members.

It may be appropriate to include representatives from the secondary schools right from the beginning, so that colleagues from both sectors meet from the start.

### REFLECTIVE TASK

It is vital to have **nominated people**, so that everyone knows whom to contact.

Liaison is likely to be more effective if it enjoys the support of senior management: get your head teacher on board.

Establish **clear lines of communication** – who communicates what, to whom, when.

Eventually your cluster will want to feed into a **larger network**, supported by an Advanced Skills or Advisory Teacher, Primary Languages Consultant for the LA, adviser or strategy manager.

Agree meeting dates well in advance and put these in the school calendar.

### What shall we talk about?

### REFLECTIVE TASK

Imagine that you are already the Primary Languages Co-ordinator in a school. You are going to meet with secondary colleagues and other feeder primaries.

- In threes, brainstorm a list of the issues about which you need to make collaborative decisions in order to implement the Primary Languages entitlement in your schools.
- What kinds of issues would you have to consider and plan for?
- Compare your findings with others in your class, drawing up a master list.

How does your list compare with the suggestions below?

- **Which language**(s) to teach.
- **Who is to do the teaching**: staffing.
- The **advantages** and **disadvantages** of different delivery models (see Chapter 2).
- When and how to make a start: which **year groups**.
- Time to be allocated to Primary Languages in the curriculum.
- **Time for staff to meet**.
- Time for teachers to become familiar with the Framework and supporting documentation.
- **What they should teach** – the Primary Languages curriculum.
- Developing long-, medium- and short-term plans, schemes of work.
- Choosing materials, including ICT resources.
- Continuity and progression.
- The need to identify best practice from primary and secondary approaches to teaching and learning.
- **Who should learn**: inclusion.
- **Beyond** the entitlement – **Early Years//Reception/Foundation**.
- Record keeping and assessment.
- Liaison and transition to secondary school.
- **Sustainability**: funding and budgetary constraints.
- Sustainability: outside school links with secondary languages teachers, LAs, regional and national agencies involved in Primary Languages.
- **Support** for your colleagues.

Remember that it is highly recommended that strategic planning related to the above issues takes place at local or even regional level.

To address these issues competently, you require information about how languages fit in to the whole of your school's priorities. A few senior managers, who recall previous failures in Primary Languages projects, have yet to be convinced of its benefits, though this is becoming rarer.

# Choosing which language(s) to teach

The Key Stage 2 Framework for Languages does **not** specify the language which you have to teach. Schools are free to choose to teach any modern or community language. Even so, the decision about which language to teach will probably be closely linked to the availability of staff in your school with particular language skills and the confidence and willingness to start teaching the language in which they have some experience or in which there is training and support.

When deciding on language choice, it is really important to work in **a cluster** and discuss with other primary schools locally what language they are teaching. Similarly, it is vital to liaise closely with your main associated secondary schools to find out what languages are taught in Key Stage 3 and how your proposed language choice fits in with their provision. Sometimes language choice is linked to the availability of visiting secondary languages specialists.

Occasionally, choice of language or delivery model depends on the language policies of your LA, as for instance in Coventry, where a specific multilingual language awareness programme has been encouraged (see Chapter 2). On the whole, however, the majority of primary schools tend to choose one language as their main language, although some offer a 2 + 2 programme, with two years of one language, followed by two years of another. Research conducted by the NFER (DCSF, 2007, 2008) indicates that French is the language most frequently chosen, partly because teachers are most likely to know some French, and partly because children are likely to begin French in Year 7, so that there is a good chance of continuity in learning, especially when most of a school's children move to the same secondary school.

**REFLECTIVE TASK**

The implications of language choice for the dominance of languages such as French and for diversification programmes at secondary level must be considered.

On the other hand, a sound case can be made for languages such as Spanish, which, as well as being easier in some respects for teachers and children to learn, is also popular with both parents and children on account of Spanish-speaking areas being a common holiday destination for some families. There are also parts of the country where a particular home language is being widely taught because this best fits the needs of the local community.

**REFLECTIVE TASK**

Whatever you decide, you need to choose a language which can be sustained and resourced, if needs be across Years 3 to 6.

There is evidence from the Scottish MLPS projects that parents may encourage their children to switch from other languages learned at primary school to French on entry to secondary school.

# Staffing

**PRACTICAL TASK** PRACTICAL TASK PRACTICAL TASK PRACTICAL TASK PRACTICAL TASK

(You need your Key Stage 2 Framework.)

- Make a note of the various staffing models which are possible, using the list in Part 2 page 6.
- Discuss what you feel are the advantages and disadvantages of the different models.

There is a useful summary of the advantages and disadvantages of using a visiting specialist, the primary class teacher and native speaker assistants in the Key Stage 2 Pathfinder evaluation (Muijs et al., 2005).

**REFLECTIVE TASK**

- As intending primary teachers, what do you feel are your particular strengths as future languages teachers?

- What are your professional development needs?
- Compare your list with those of other trainees.

**REFLECTIVE TASK**

Encourage colleagues to think about the **skills they already have as expert primary practitioners** and which they bring with them to language teaching. How would you ensure that this occurs?

# Further human resources to complement language teachers

The National Languages Strategy suggests that children should have access to native speakers. One possibility is to use native speaker assistants, of which there are various categories:

- native speakers with qualified teacher status;
- Foreign Language Assistants (FLAs);
- trainee teachers from abroad;
- members of the community.

FLAs generally do not intend to be teachers, but are students spending time in England as part of their studies, with the intention of improving their English. Other young native speakers, who may intend to be teachers, are Comenius language assistants who come over to spend time in English schools. You can find out more about deploying a native speaker in Martin with Farren (2006) and from the British Council.

(Making contact with native speakers in any of the above categories may also inspire you to make links abroad and create an international dimension for the whole school.)

**REFLECTIVE TASK**

Native speakers and FLAs require specific support mechanisms. Discuss what these might be.

Your audit may also reveal that you have teaching assistants or HLTAs with language skills who would be happy to participate in Primary Languages teaching, given appropriate support and training. If you go to www.primarylanguages.org.uk you can view some very effective work being done by teaching assistants.

# When to make a start towards full entitlement

There are a number of possibilities related to where best to set up your provision, if you are short of staff, which can be summed up as deciding on whether to work

- Top down       Year 6?       Year 5/6 (QCA schemes of work 2000)
or
- Bottom up       Year 3? (Key Stage 2 Framework/QCA schemes of work 2007)
- Beyond the entitlement? (Early Years/Reception/Foundation; extra–curricular clubs and events)

The Key Stage 2 Pathfinder evaluation team (DfES, 2005) found that many schools were making a start in Year 6 and working backwards down through Year 5 as time went on, or that they prioritised the top two years of Key Stage 2, as these were closest to the Key Stage 3 transition point, and had also been the year groups supported by the original QCA schemes of work (2000). In fact, in practical terms this was tricky to implement as regards planning, and a preferred option seemed to be to start teaching in Year 3 and to work upwards in a cumulative way, year on year.

Sometimes schools start in Year 3 but do not offer any languages in the years above, building on the next year with just Years 3 and 4, then Years 3, 4, and 5 and finally all four Years 3–6. Doing so leaves some year groups without languages lessons for a considerable time.

An alternative is for all Key Stage 2 teachers to attend the Year 3 training and then all to teach their own classes, but using the Year 3 resources in the first year of operation, perhaps with some different songs and stories for the older learners but basically using the same materials throughout the school. In the second year, the new Year 3 children are introduced to Year 3 work, but other year groups and their teachers are trained and work with Year 4 resources and so on.

Here is an example from a school in the north of England, which is working with *Early Start* resources, and has planned to phase these in over a number of years:

| 2005–2006 | | | 2006–2007 | | |
|---|---|---|---|---|---|
| Y3 | *Early Start 1* | Units 1–8 | Y3 | *Early Start 1* | Units 1–8 |
| Y4 | *Early Start 1* | Units 1–8 | Y4 | *Early Start 1* | Units 9–16 |
| Y5 | *Early Start 1* | Units 1–8 | Y5 | *Early Start 1* | Units 9–16 |
| Y6 | *Early Start 1* | Units 1–8 | Y6 | *Early Start 1* | Units 9–16 |

| 2007–2008 | | | 2008–2009 | | |
|---|---|---|---|---|---|
| Y3 | *Early Start 1* | Units 1–8 | Y3 | *Early Start 1* | Units 1–8 |
| Y4 | *Early Start 1* | Units 9–16 | Y4 | *Early Start 1* | Units 9–16 |
| Y5 | *Early Start 2* | Units 1–8 | Y5 | *Early Start 2* | Units 1–8 |
| Y6 | *Early Start 2* | Units 1–8 | Y6 | *Early Start 2* | Units 9–16 |

# Key Stage 1

Currently the Primary Languages entitlement as part of the National Languages Strategy is only for Key Stage 2. However, schools are also free to develop language teaching in Key Stage 1 and may choose to offer an encounter with several languages or make an early start to the language which will be learned in Key Stage 2.

*Languages in Key Stage 1 can help:*
- *build links between school and home, especially where children are speakers of other languages;*
- *develop listening and speaking skills and build confidence;*
- *encourage and develop children's linguistic and creative skills;*

- *build positive attitudes to languages and culture;*
- *develop learning about other countries and cultures.*

(DfES, 2005, Part 2, p9)

You can find guidance about introducing languages into Key Stage 1 in the Key Stage 2 Framework, (DfES, 2005, Part 3:6, pp86–89).

---

**REFLECTIVE TASK**

if your school has the expertise and resources to offer languages in Key Stage 1, **then this must be acknowledged and built on at the start of Key Stage 2**.

If your school is starting from a low baseline and making a more tentative start, it is important **not to be distracted** by offering languages in Key Stage 1 and spreading your resources (human and material) too thinly, with the result that the Key Stage 2 entitlement is affected.

---

# Time: fitting Primary Languages into the curriculum

The Key Stage 2 Framework is based on schools teaching Primary Languages for an hour a week within curriculum time. This is the area, about which teachers and head teachers have most concerns – how to fit Primary Languages into the busy curriculum. You need to make clear that the hour a week suggested **does not** imply a single long lesson once a week, although sometimes this is what happens, particularly when a visiting teacher is delivering the teaching.

The hour can be divided into a number of shorter lessons, for example two 30-minute lessons, three 20-minute lessons, or 10 or 15 minutes daily. As we noted in Chapter 4 on planning, even short sessions need to be well planned and not simply 'happen'.

## Finding additional time – embedding and integrating Primary Languages

In addition to these discrete lessons, you can find additional time for languages by integrating languages work into the remainder of the primary curriculum as much as possible. As well as this, you can encourage and support colleagues to incorporate languages into daily classroom routines. For example, using the new language to greet children, give instructions, praise, and in everyday classroom language such as 'stand up', 'hands up'. Your copy of the QCA schemes of work and trainee support materials provide you with lots of examples of how to do this.

---

**REFLECTIVE TASK**

Integration and embedding, together with CLIL approaches, offer a potential increase in intensity of the new language. These approaches are difficult to implement if the class teacher is not the languages teacher. How would you support this happening?

---

## A note about PPA time

Since the introduction of PPA time, many schools have turned to PPA as a way of finding time for Primary Languages. Where this happens, the teaching is often done by a visiting teacher, sometimes an outreach teacher from a secondary school, and sometimes by a visiting primary specialist, or even an in-house specialist, who uses the PPA time to teach in colleagues' classes.

In some respects this is a practical solution to several 'problems' over fitting languages in. However, often (because it is PPA time), there are no class teachers present during the languages lessons. This has real repercussions for the ability of the normal class teacher to continue with the languages teaching throughout the week or to be 'trained' through watching and participating, as another (specialist) teacher teaches. It also mitigates against the shared professional understandings which are so empowering.

In addition to time for teaching, allow **time for planning** and ensure adequate **lead-in time** for whatever you are intending to develop.

Build in time for:

- **training** primary teachers in languages methodology and secondary teachers in primary pedagogy;
- **evaluating** and learning lessons from any previous collaboration;
- **reviewing** current initiatives.

# Primary Languages curriculum – what should be taught?

You will find a discussion on the different aims and purposes for Primary Languages learning and the linked teaching approaches in Chapter 2. Briefly, you have to decide on one or a combination of the following.

- Multilingual language **awareness**.
- **Encounter/sensitisation**.
- Language **competence**.
- **Continuum** with a change of focus as children move through the key stage.

Planning and resourcing, recording and reporting have been considered in previous chapters. You can find advice on planning for mixed-age classes in the *Teacher's guide* for the QCA schemes of work and in the Framework Part 3: 8, p117 *Using the Framework in different contexts*. As you consider these issues, take into account the information generated by the audit. Your fellow teachers are likely to have priorities and pressures aside from languages.

# Recording for transition purposes

As Primary Languages Co-ordinator seek to find out what links your school already has with secondary schools in the vicinity. Is there a whole school transition policy at all? Do Year 6 teachers have any contact with secondary teachers? What information, if any, is transferred? Does this take the form that is most helpful for secondary colleagues? Do they actually use it? Is there something else that would be preferable – but still manageable?

A simple child profile for languages devised by Malcolm Hope former MFL adviser in Oxfordshire looks similar to this:

| Primary Languages assessment profile | John Smith Y6 | Name of school |
|---|---|---|
| | Weak | Strong |
| Oracy | | ————————————————X— |
| Literacy | | —————————————X————————— |
| Intercultural Understanding | | ——————————X————————— |
| Knowledge about Language | | ———————X——————————— |
| Language Learning Strategies | | ——————————X————————— |

Remember that secondary departments in Key Stage 3 will only be able to review their languages provision to take account of what children already know, understand and can do, if they receive appropriate information.

# Inclusion: equal opportunities in languages learning

The National Curriculum Statutory Inclusion Statement (2000) sets out three key principles:
  A. *Setting suitable learning challenges*
  B. *Responding to pupils' diverse learning needs*
  C. *Overcoming potential barriers to learning and assessment for individuals and groups of pupils*

The Primary Languages entitlement is inclusive and makes a valuable contribution to the principles above as well as to the Every Child Matters agenda. The Framework supports equality of opportunity for all children, including those with special educational needs or disabilities, gifted and talented children, and children for whom English is a second or additional language. There is a good deal of evidence from across the country that children with special educational needs typically respond positively and enthusiastically to practical, interactive language lessons based mainly on speaking and listening. Primary languages lessons can provide a great opportunity for all children to reinforce social skills such as turn taking, working with a talk partner, playing a team game and listening to the views and experiences of others. Although some newly arrived EAL children's proficiency in English may influence the proportion of instructions you give in English in a languages lesson, children for whom English is an additional language are often proud to see languages other than English being celebrated within Primary Languages lessons and may be skilled language learners themselves, on account of their plurilingualism.

**PRACTICAL TASK** PRACTICAL TASK PRACTICAL TASK PRACTICAL TASK PRACTICAL TASK

(You need your Key Stage 2 Framework.)

Read Part 3, pages 47–63 entitled *Inclusion – languages for all.*

- Allocate different sections to different trainees within your group (for example, page 47 Special Educational Needs (SEN) children, pages 53–55 strategies for support, pages 57–58 Gifted and Talented children, page 59 EAL children).
- Report on the chosen section to each other.
- How do these approaches compare with what you have experienced in your placement schools?

# Mutual support

Chapter 9 details sources of support, but perhaps one of the key messages which you will want to stress as a Primary Languages Co-ordinator is that of **working in partnership** with each other, sharing resources, ideas, personnel (teachers and assistants), achievements and anxieties. Planning together enables the linguistic expertise of the secondary specialist and some of the pedagogy to complement the creativity, imagination and skill of the primary teacher.

If planning together throughout Key Stage 2 is beyond your resources, perhaps some of the Year 6 work could be jointly planned with receiving Year 7 teachers. Your collaboration might go further and you could actually undertake some **co-teaching** in Year 6 and Year 7. If some of your colleagues are initially anxious about a long-term arrangement, how about a two-week unit planned and taught collaboratively at the end of the summer term of Year 6?

You may wish to consider a **bridging unit** or an activity which crosses the transition and brings children and teachers into contact with each other. You could start small with a shared morning or afternoon post National Tests. Compliment each other through a 'showing and sharing' day. The annual **European Day of Languages** on 26 September could be an opportunity for collaboration. Some schools run language or cultural festivals, others share performances such as music, drama or sport. Perhaps primary and secondary teachers could work in pairs in a buddy system? Could the secondary school(s) offer a summer school or taster lessons?

**Mutual lesson observation** between primary and secondary teachers produces gains on both sides and enhances the secondary teachers' ability to build on children's prior learning, based on a deeper understanding and knowledge of what really happens in primary schools today. Primary teachers also benefit from more knowledge about what will be expected of children, when they move up to secondary school, especially as regards skills and pace.

## REFLECTIVE TASK

Visits – in both directions – need to have a clear focus and purpose.

Could Primary Languages teachers, secondary languages teachers and literacy/English specialists from Key Stages 2 and 3 work together to identify skills which are common to language learning, regardless of language? What about identifying areas of common practice across schemes of work, and providing a common glossary of terms? This would benefit learners by providing a coherence of teaching approach.

Pedagogical continuity of teaching approach across the transition between primary and secondary school should be ensured.

Children from Year 6 and Year 7 can be paired in a buddy system, or students in Year 7 who have previously learned the new language can be paired with children who have not.

If children in Year 6 do a bridging unit or have other examples of work, these can contribute to a display in both the primary and the secondary school, which demonstrates to new Year 7 children that their earlier languages learning is valued.

Some schools have used secondary students as ambassadors in primary schools; working towards their Young Leaders Award, they have done some teaching in primary. Other schools have organised joint visits abroad, and others contacts via video conferencing.

# Sustainability

## Budgetary constraints

Your responsibilities may include managing a budget for Primary Languages in your school. If there is not one, request a **specific budget allocation**. You need to consider money not just for resources, including software and other classroom equipment, but for continuing professional development (CPD) for yourself and colleagues (some ideas follow in Chapter 9) and for supply cover arrangements, including for time for meeting together. Check with your LA about Standards funding and how much your school has been allocated.

## Supporting staff

Your Primary Languages Co-ordinator role may include addressing training needs: pedagogic and linguistic. It may involve leading staff meetings, helping with language upskilling, providing training for software, organising some joint primary and secondary INSET. If you encourage colleagues to attend or if you organise twilight sessions, consider a brisk start and early and prompt finish times, as teachers will be tired (and so will you, if you are delivering the training yourself). E-learning is another form of training, which is becoming increasingly possible with new technologies. Whatever form the support takes, you need to be sensitive to concerns teachers have about their pronunciation, rusty grammar or lack of first-hand cultural experience. Remember, one-off training can kick-start a project, but in order to build capacity and achieve sustainability, it is essential to ensure **ongoing support**. As a Primary Languages Co-ordinator you will always have new teachers to train, support and encourage, but do not forget to consolidate those who have already started. Chapter 9 offers you support in tackling these circumstances.

Training should **build on primary school strengths and pedagogy** and not import a secondary model into primary.

In order to be able to carry out this support role, you will need to attend subject leader meetings or INSET offered by your LA, so that you can cascade any relevant information on staff development days or at staff meetings. The following are some guidelines for success-ful cluster and network working.

- Create opportunities for **adult learning**.
- Identify skills, experience, expertise of cluster/network members, and keep a **central record**.
- Consider arranging **demo lessons** by a primary Advanced Skills Teacher (AST) or Languages Consultant.
- **Record some lessons** on video for joint viewing/training.
- **Balance internal and external expertise** – sometimes having too many outside speakers or experts can actually be disempowering.
- Ask cluster/network members to **feedback** on training events.
- Hold meetings in **different** schools.
- Involve **newer teachers and TAs** who may have important contributions to make.
- Ensure a sense of **collective ownership** and leadership by rotating some tasks.
- Expect members to contribute and lead on **sub-tasks** as a means of developing wider leadership potential.
- Consider using **school websites** to publish outcomes.
- Mutually agree on **key milestones** and success criteria.

# Writing a languages policy for your school/ Contributing to the School Development Plan

It will probably be your task to create or amend a Primary Languages Policy for your school. This is one means of ensuring that work in languages becomes part of a whole school commitment to language development. In other words, you will be articulating for collea-gues, governors, parents, the LA, Ofsted what your vision for Primary Languages in your school is and how this is to be achieved. The policy will draw on all the factors we have discussed above.

## REFLECTIVE TASK

- Bearing in mind the themes in the preceding chapters, brainstorm together the kinds of information you feel a Languages Policy for a school ought to include.
- Compare your lists with the contents of actual policies and the suggestions below.

Most of the headings you will need have been covered either in this chapter or elsewhere in this book. You can find suggestions for *Aims and purposes of Primary Languages* in the QCA Teacher's Guide, page 4. You might need to add to these any details of specific local circumstances affecting your school. There are examples of language policies on the NACELL website.

It is a good idea if a policy shows what the Primary Languages Co-ordinator's role is. Below is an extract from a policy.

The Primary Languages Co-ordinator will facilitate the development of Primary Languages by:

○ managing the implementation of the Primary Languages policy;
○ updating the policy and scheme of work;
○ ordering/updating/allocating resources;
○ identifying need and arranging INSET so that staff are confident in how to teach and assess Primary Languages and have sufficient subject knowledge;
○ keeping staff abreast of new developments;
○ taking an overview of whole school planning to ensure that there is continuity between year groups and that progression is taking place;
○ supporting staff in developing children's capability;
○ attending appropriate courses to update knowledge of current developments and links with the Advisory Team for MFL;
○ contributing to the School Development Plan on an annual basis;
○ managing the native speaker if available;
○ liaising with other primary and secondary schools in the cluster;
○ reviewing this policy annually.

A major review involving all staff will take place every three years.

**REFLECTIVE TASK**

Your school colleagues will have greater ownership of a Languages Policy if, rather than simply handing a ready written languages policy over to them, you involve them in its creation, writing it with them, even if you start with the headings and take final responsibility for the completion of the document. Be cautious about forecasting outcomes.

As well as a languages policy and the more formal channels of a School Development Plan, it is helpful to keep parents, governors and members of the wider community informed through newsletters. This raises the profile of Primary Languages on a regular basis.

# The characteristics of an excellent Primary Languages Co-ordinator

Ros Venables defines the characteristics of a subject leader as follows:

A leader:

● takes a strategic view;
● has vision and articulates it;
● creates a collaborative culture and develops the staff;
● reviews the status quo and constantly seeks to improve it;
● responds to developments and needs;
● has excellent working relationships with colleagues;
● is keen to develop their own subject knowledge;
● sets an example which others seek to follow;

- helps develop other colleagues' subject knowledge;
- expects high standards;
- has and communicates a clear set of educational values.

Putting your vision for Primary Languages into practice needs to be a three-stage process as depicted in the plan-do-review cycle below.

**Think: Plan – do – review as a cycle**

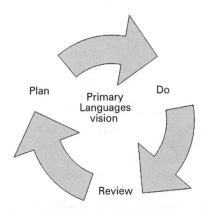

Plan

Primary
Languages
vision

Do

Review

## A SUMMARY OF **KEY POINTS**

> The transition to secondary languages teaching should be viewed as part of a coherent 7–14 whole, rather than as separate primary and secondary languages programmes.

> Head and senior managers need to support Primary Languages initiatives.

> Working in cross-phase clusters and networks is highly recommended.

> Nominate co-ordinators for clusters and networks to simplify communication: this role can be rotated.

> There should be shared and equitable discussions: primary projects should not be secondary 'led'.

> Focus on transferable skills relevant to L1, home languages, first and second foreign languages.

> Continuers must be valued: a clean slate approach is very demotivating.

> Start small – learn, listen, review, encourage feedback.

> Spread the message, involve and inform governors, parents, local community.

> Use technology to support language refresher courses and resource exchanges and virtual communities of practice.

**MOVING** *ON* > > > > > > MOVING *ON* > > > > > > MOVING *ON*

As a Primary Languages Co-ordinator you need to constantly update your own subject knowledge in order to lead and inspire others, helping them find the support they require. Chapter 9 will give you more information on how to set about this task. Make it a point during your training period, and your NQT year, to seek out courses, conferences and training opportunities for yourself to help equip you for this role. Perhaps your career entry and development profile (CEDP) and Induction targets could include aspects related to your Primary Languages Co-ordinator role?

**FURTHER READING** FURTHER READING **FURTHER READING** FURTHER READING

Bolster, A., Balandier-Brown, C. and Rea-Dickins, P. (2004) Young learners of modern foreign languages and their transition to the secondary phase: a lost opportunity? *Language Learning Journal*, Winter 2004 (30) 35–41.

DfES (2005) Key *Stage 2 Framework for Languages Part 2 Section 5: Supporting primary entitlement*. This is essential reading, as it contains advice on working in partnership and supporting transition and therefore building for the future. Nottingham: DfES Publications.

Jones, J. and Coffey, S. (2006) Transition from primary to secondary – continuity, cohesion and progresson, in Jones, J. and Coffey, S. (2006) *Modern Languages 5-11*. London: David Fulton Publishers.

## Useful websites

QCA website: Pathways to learning for new arrivals pages include a specific MFL section explaining how language classes are able to raise the self-esteem of new arrivals with very limited English; providing an opportunity for community languages to contribute linguistic and cultural knowledge and to become involved in classes www.qca.org.uk/qca_7525.aspx

**Respect for all** pages provide guidance on the potential of National Curriculum subjects, including MFL, for valuing diversity and challenging racism – www.qca.org.uk/

www.bbc.co.uk/languages/ – has language courses to help upskill teachers, as well as materials for young language learners

www.lclclubs.com/babelzonenew – mirrors much of the work set out in the QCA schemes of work and contains numerous sound files related to each unit which can be used for teachers to gain confidence in the target language; these are free to access online

www.specialeducationneeds.com – has information and resources for teachers and children with a wide range of special educational needs; also has links to other sources of information

# 9
# Looking forward: becoming a Primary Languages professional

By the end of this chapter you will have:

- become aware of the most important sources of support for yourself and your primary colleagues;
- learned how to access further professional development through courses in the UK and abroad;
- appreciated the benefits of joining a professional association.

This chapter addresses the following Professional Standards for QTS:
Q6, Q7a, Q7b, Q6, Q8. Q9, Q14, Q15, Q32, Q33

As you reach the end of the ITT course, you need to be planning for your professional future. You will do this partly through the completion of your Career Entry Development Profile and the creation of targets and areas of interest and development for your induction year.

As someone with a specialism in Primary Languages, you are likely to find yourself almost immediately in what may start off by being an informal leadership role, as the new curriculum area Primary Languages comes on stream around 2010. So, although you may still be an NQT, or a relatively inexperienced teacher, schools will find you a useful resource.

We considered some of the areas about which you might have to make decisions in the earlier chapter on Subject Leadership. In this chapter we want to consider how you can access support specifically related to Primary Languages for yourself and colleagues.

Part 2 of the Key Stage 2 Framework for Languages lists various sources of support and further information. The most important are summed up below.

# Developing your subject knowledge

Specialist knowledge is a characteristic of a profession and developing your knowledge, skills and understanding beyond the level needed to qualify as a teacher is a long-term process. As a beginning teacher, you will be developing your subject skills in the context of a wide range of new professional demands, including teaching the whole of the National Curriculum. Continuing to develop your subject specialism is a particular challenge in your first year of teaching, but you can tackle this strategically and this final chapter offers a range of suggestions for keeping up to date and inspired.

## Further study

As part of your ITT, you are increasingly likely to have written some assignments at Masters level and to have thereby gained part of a higher level qualification. It is a good idea to find out if there are any Early Professional Development modules available as part of further

Masters' level qualifications. Sometimes you can begin to investigate a topic which really interests you as early as your final teaching placement or start preparation during your NQT year. And even if you do not wish to continue reading and writing in such depth, there are many possibilities for lower level professional courses as part of CPD, some accredited and others not (details are below).

At the very least you can keep up with developments in Primary Languages and broader educational issues through *The Times Educational Supplement* and *Guardian Education* or through a publication like *Primary Subjects,* which is distributed to all maintained primary schools (currently free of charge).

# Professional associations and other organisations

## Association for Language Learning

Joining a professional association demonstrates that you take your professional development as a new teacher seriously. The Association for Language Learning (ALL) is the major subject association in the UK for teachers of all languages at all levels, keeping you up to date and well informed on all that is happening in languages. What is important about ALL is that it is an entirely independent voice for everyone involved in languages in whatever sector. It therefore has an advocacy and representative role and is able to take concerns forward. It also enables you to join a network of other enthusiastic professionals. It is not, however, in any way a teachers' union.

At the time of writing, membership for primary teachers costs just £20 per year and offers you a range of benefits, as well as being a means of putting you in direct touch with experienced enthusiasts in Primary Languages. Why not enquire whether you can have your subscription and attendance at the annual conference included in your professional development plan? This will give you access to talks and workshops directly related to Primary Languages, and allow you to share ideas with teachers from other schools and parts of the country. Conference exhibitions display the latest books and resources, including ICT, and access to the exhibitions is usually free of charge. Currently, the ALL, at www.all-languages.org.uk, offers free membership, and some day places at its annual conference, to newly qualified teachers. You will also be allocated to an ALL branch or network of your choice. These meet early evening or sometimes on a Saturday morning. There are also language committees which you might like to get involved in. Newcomers are always more than welcome and ALL is especially keen to support Primary Languages teachers.

## National Advisory Centre on Early Language Learning: NACELL

After joining a professional association, your next port of call should be NACELL, which was created in 1999 as part of the DfES Early Language Learning Initiative. As you will already be aware, NACELL is a physical resource in the sense that you can visit it at CILT headquarters in London and browse through a range of publications and materials for young language learners. In addition, NACELL is a virtual source of online support, which you can access through the website on www.nacell.org.uk and which will eventually be available via www.primarylanguages.org.uk. You are sure to have been looking at the NACELL website throughout your initial teacher training programme, but as an emerging professional, you need to be familiar with particular parts of the site. Here are the current headings for sections listed on the home page:

- Home page;
- What you're doing;
- Ideas for the classroom;
- Best practice guide;
- Official documentation;
- Regional support;
- Resources;
- Professional development;
- Networking;
- Site map.

**PRACTICAL TASK** PRACTICAL TASK PRACTICAL TASK PRACTICAL TASK PRACTICAL TASK

(You will need internet access to the NACELL website.)

Open the NACELL homepage or go to the NACELL section of the www.primarylanguages.org.uk.

- One of you should take responsibility for summing up the latest news on the home page. Each of the other members of your group should take responsibility for looking at one of the sections listed.

- Spend some time looking at the section you have been allocated, and then report back to each other on key features or new items in your section.

### Regional and local support – NACELL Regional Support Groups

You may already have attended some Regional Support Group (RSG) sessions as part of your training programme, but if not, these are a key source of support, networking, and practical ideas on a whole range of topics. Even if your first teaching post is in an area of the country quite different from your initial teacher training institution, you are bound to find a NACELL RSG near you. ELL RSGs are managed by the nine Comenius Centres, and each has one or more co-ordinators who organise a programme of five twilight sessions free of charge each year. You can find details of these sessions on the NACELL website and also brief reports of sessions already held to give you a flavour of the kinds of things to expect. Each RSG has a character of its own and you will always be very welcome. If you are a Primary Languages Co-ordinator, you will find that RSGs are a good place to start to encourage some of your class teacher colleagues to attend sessions and get support. There is no requirement to attend all sessions – it is not like signing up for a course – although all RSGs have some members who attend every session offered! There is a social feel to RSGs, with each meeting preceded by refreshments and time built in for sharing, getting to know each other and generally finding support.

# Primary Strategy Learning Networks

Primary Strategy Learning Networks encourage groups of primary schools to work together with a focus on a common subject in order to raise standards. Consult www.standards. dfes.gov.uk/primary/publications/learning_networks/1095729.

## Association for Language Learning Primary Special Interest Group

The ALL has a Primary Special Interest Group which offers a 'phone a friend' service in order to support Primary Languages teachers. Contact the ALL office at www.all-languages.org.uk to find out more. The Primary Special Interest Group represents ALL primary views on a number of national bodies and has responded to the primary element of the Dearing Review of the 14–19 curriculum, the Primary Review consultations led by Robin Alexander and the Rose Review of the primary curriculum. It also works to publish resources collaboratively with other subject association partners, including the Primary Project Box for Key Stage 1, which is a cross-curricular set of materials, including units for Primary Languages. It contributes to the *Primary Subjects* magazine (see below).

# Further sources of support

## CILT Comenius Key Stage 2 Language Consultants

Each of the nine Comenius regions of the country has one or two part-time Comenius Key Stage 2 Language Consultants, who may be able to help you and your school or cluster to set up or sustain Primary Languages development. The Comenius manager for the region in which you are working will be able to put you in touch if this is appropriate and you can find their details on the NACELL website.

## Early Language Learning – Language College programme

The ELL-LC programme managed by CILT, has been encouraging language colleges to work with their feeder primaries for some years now and there are currently over 250 specialist language colleges (SLCs) involved with this project. You can find out more on www.cilt.org.uk/languagecolleges/projects/projects.htm. In any case, all language colleges have funds for primary outreach work. CILT Language Teaching Advisers work with clusters of participating SLCs and primary partners to run local and regional seminars and conferences across the country. This year's focus is progression through the Key Stage 2 Framework and planning for transition. There is a major annual dissemination conference for SLCs and their primary partners. Each LA has at least one SLC, and some have responsibility for Primary Languages throughout the authority.

## Regional trainers for the Key Stage 2 Framework

A few years ago the Department for Children, Schools and Families commissioned CILT to train a cohort of national trainers to train others to deliver the Key Stage 2 Framework under an initiative called the Training the Trainers programme. These national trainers in turn have trained cohorts of regional trainers, usually working through networks with delegates nominated by LAs. The regional trainers are now working with their local partners, often SLCs, secondary and primary schools, ASTs and consultants. You can find out who your local trainer is by contacting Philip.harding@cilt.org.uk.

# Local authorities

Each LA has received some Standards funding to help support the development of Primary Languages locally. Many have their own Primary Languages Consultants or advisory teachers and Advanced Skills Teachers whose role is to help you with queries and advice and often to deliver training, both external for groups of teachers and sometimes in-house for your school or cluster.

## British Council – Foreign Language Assistants

There is now a well-established scheme for FLAs within the primary school which is managed by the British Council. To find out more look at www.britishcouncil.org/languageassistants.htm. Native speakers can enrich the teaching of languages in the primary phase as they bring the language alive and have first-hand knowledge of the cultural context, as well as supporting teachers' confidence in speaking and understanding the language. You can work with two or three other primary schools to employ an FLA or share one with a secondary school. The British Council produce resources to support FLAs in primary schools produced by the British Council and guidance can be found in other publications (see reference list).

# Conferences and exhibitions

## The Primary Languages Show

The major event of the Primary Languages year is the Primary Languages Show which has been running since 1996, usually in Manchester, although the venue is likely to change owing to the huge size and success of the event. This two-day conference happens every spring, at the end of February or beginning of March, and is a blend of plenaries and more strategic presentations on the Friday and dozens of workshops on both days, especially Saturday. The programme is packed with practical activities and there is also a large free exhibition of the growing number of resources of every kind available for Primary Languages.

## Language World

Language World, the annual two-day conference of the ALL, is held in a variety of venues across the country. In recent years, the conference has been held in Oxford. This event is not just for Primary Languages but for all language professionals in all settings from primary right through secondary, post-16, adult and higher education, bringing together practitioners, policy makers, teacher trainers, information specialists and trainees. But there are always workshops on primary themes – in 2008, for example, one of Saturday's key themes was the transition from primary to secondary school. Again, there is a large free exhibition which includes resources for Primary Languages. It is well worthwhile putting both events in your diary.

## Free exhibitions

The Languages Show held in Olympia in November and the British Educational Technology Exhibition (BETT) in January offer free seminars and exhibits of a wide range of resources for teaching languages. Both are in London, and open on Saturday. The Education Show, in February or March in Birmingham, has similar scope. Exhibitions sponsored by a single publisher can be informative, but it is as well to remember that publishers promote their own products.

# Courses

## UK courses

As you will have discovered through the practical task on page 133, through the NACELL website you will find details of a range of CPD courses organised by CILT. Some of these are one-day courses, specifically for Primary Languages. Obviously the themes and titles of the courses change from year to year, but there are usually taster courses in a variety of languages for teachers without much confidence in language teaching. There are also courses for different languages for different National Curriculum year groups, with a particular focus on aspects of the Key Stage 2 Framework for Languages. You will find that there are courses suitable for beginner teachers in languages who lack experience and expertise and need reassurance, as well as training for more established Primary Languages practitioners, who have been teaching languages for some time in schools and are seeking professional development to help both themselves and children's progress. There are also conferences, courses and support for teachers of Community Languages.

## Courses abroad

### CILT

CILT produces a brochure with CPD opportunities abroad – there are one-week and two-week summer courses in France, Spain and Germany, each designed with a different audience in mind. Each course is a lively mix of language enhancement classes and practical workshops. A number of these courses attract grants towards the cost of attendance available through the Comenius professional development programme, managed by the British Council, so that in the end, the cost to the teacher is small.

### British Council

The British Council is the United Kingdom's international organisation for cultural relations and educational opportunities. Visit its website at www.britishcouncil.org.uk for details of visits and courses abroad as well as school exchanges for children.

Another form of on-the-job training is provided by the **2-Week Primary Teachers' Project** for primary school teachers engaged in language teaching at Key Stage 2. Teachers are recruited by regional co-ordinators, usually in groups of ten, to attend training that incorporates one week of language tuition in their target language and one week of job shadowing in a school in the country of that language. This programme targets EU Comenius funding plus a DCSF supply contribution per teacher (for schools in England) so that participating teachers pay a very reduced contribution indeed. As someone leading on delivering Primary Languages in your school, this professional development could well be for you, especially if you want first-hand knowledge of the country provided by the school placement and the cultural programme, as well as improved language skills. The programme is also open to other primary teachers involved in teaching languages, as well as teaching assistants and HLTAs. Most group visits occur close to half term in either the winter, spring or summer terms. Contact the British Council to find out the deadlines, which are several months ahead of the various departure dates. The co-ordinator will support you completing the application forms and you will meet other teachers from your region through the programme.

### Le français en Ecosse

Funding is also available from the European Union Comenius Lifelong Learning Programme administered by the British Council for some immersion style courses run by *Le français en Ecosse.* Each year teachers from all over Europe have the opportunity to attend courses in France to develop their discursive skills, update their methodology and exchange ideas for good practice in the classroom. You can find out more at www.lfee.net and read comments from past participants. The grant fully covers the course fee, subsistence and accommodation, as well as travel expenses.

### Global Gateway

The Global Gateway at www.globalgateway.org.uk offers opportunities to make international partnerships with schools around the world, and provides wider cultural information about other countries and global citizenship. Perhaps you could find a school partner or even go for an International School Award.

# Publications to support Primary Languages

In addition to conferences, courses and regional support networks, there are many publications aimed at the professional development of teachers, from which you can gain support. CILT publishes a range of practical and inexpensive books entitled *Young Pathfinders* and *Resourcefiles* which are useful to have both personally and also for the staffroom for consultation by class teachers.

## *Primary Languages*

The ALL has been working in partnership with all the other subject associations, and supported by the DCSF, to produce a series of termly magazines, which are aimed at helping subject leaders in their support role for other teachers. Look out for these in the staffroom or ask your head teacher if they have arrived. The first issue was at Easter 2008 and there is one magazine per term, entitled *Primary Subjects.* Each *Primary Subjects* folder is brightly coloured and attractive and includes A4 pamphlets from each of 16 subject associations, so you will find guidance and suggestions for teaching across the curriculum. All magazines are linked to a common theme, and in the *Primary Subjects* folder you will find a *Primary Languages* issue with practical suggestions for the development of languages in primary schools. www.subjectassociation.org.uk

## *Language Learning Journal*

There is a special 2009 edition of the ALL's journal *The Language Learning Journal*, which is devoted to Primary Languages.

# Further online support

## *Primary Languages Direct Ezine*

in January 2008 the first edition of a new free termly *ezine* was launched by CILT for everyone involved in Primary Languages. This replaced the ELL Bulletins which were launched in 1999 and used to be published termly both online and as hard copy. The *Primary Languages Direct Ezine* includes up-to-date information on resources, teaching ideas and developments, taken especially from teachers in school and key partners. All you have to do to receive it is subscribe online.

## Training Zone

If you have been working through earlier chapters, you will have accessed the Primary Languages Training Zone, which is being added to all the time. It will always be worthwhile exploring the Training Zone regularly throughout your career, in order to discover what the latest additions are. You can also use the video clips as training material to encourage and support your primary colleagues.

## Teachers' TV

You will probably also be familiar with Teachers' TV which you can access via www. teachers.tv/. Here you will find examples of Primary Languages lessons, which again you can view or download for training purposes.

## ELL-forum

In addition to the Training Zone and the CILT website, there are various discussion forums which you can join for free. The main one is the Early Language Learning forum, where you will find posted enquiries from teachers across the country on a whole host of issues together with ideas and solutions from practitioners.

## ALLnet

Membership of ALL gives you access to the ALL's weekly email distribution list, ALLnet, providing regular news and updates on local and national events being put on by ALL. If you are near London, the ALL-London branch is very vibrant.

## Qualifications and Curriculum Authority

The QCA at www.qca.org.uk has advice about all curriculum subjects. If you go to the MFL: Key Stages 1 and 2 and primary modern foreign languages pages on the QCA website, you will find guidance, resources and links for teaching Primary Languages.

## QCA Key Stage 2 scheme of work for languages

In July 2007, the QCA produced new schemes of work for Key Stage 2 French, German and Spanish which are closely linked to the Key Stage 2 Framework for Languages. These are advisory rather than statutory documents which schools can adapt for their own purposes, and are designed to be used flexibly.

The Teacher's guide and new Key Stage 2 French, German and Spanish schemes of work are available to download from www.standards.dcsf.gov.uk/schemes.

## Training and Development Agency (TDA)

If you go to www.tda.gov.uk you will find information about how to train to be a Primary Languages teacher and also information about managing your professional development. In collaboration with CILT, the TDA has supported the production of teacher trainee support material especially designed to help teacher trainees plan using the QCA schemes of work for Key Stage 2 languages. These are very suitable for use with fellow teachers as well as for yourself.

## Ofsted

The Office for Standards in Education has produced reports and materials to support the delivery of the National Languages Strategy, for example:

- *Implementing Languages Entitlement in Primary Schools*
- *Guidance on Inspecting Languages in Schools 3–11* (www.ofsted.gov.uk/assets/2978.pdf)
- *Primary Modern Foreign Languages in Initial Teacher Training – a Survey* (www.ofsted.gov.uk/assets/3424.pdf)

## National Curriculum

The National Curriculum online website has details of the non-statutory guidelines for Primary Languages at www.nc.uk.net/nc_resources/html/MFL_k2.shtml.

## National Curriculum in Action

The National Curriculum in Action website uses children's work and case studies to show what the National Curriculum in languages looks like in practice. See www.ncaction.org.uk/subjects/mfl/index.htm.

## Standards website: Department for Children, Schools and Families

The Standards website hosts the details of the Primary National Strategy and wider curricular advice. Here you can find schemes of work for primary French, German and Spanish and information on how to support children with SEN with their speaking, listening and learning skills. Go to www.standards.dcsf.gov.uk/primary or www.standards.dcsf.gov.uk/www.standards.dcsf.gov.uk/primary/languages

## Embassies and cultural institutes

Cultural institutes are a good source of information, advice and materials.
French: www.institut-francais.org.uk
German: www.goethe.de/ins/gb/lon/enindex.htm
Spanish: http://spain.embassyhomepage.com/
Italian: www.italcultur.org.uk
Japanese: www.jpf.org.uk
Chinese: www.chinese-embassy.org.uk/eng/

## Joe Dale

Head of Languages at Nodehill Middle School, Isle of Wight, Joe Dale has a blog http://joedale.typepad.com which provides practical information and guidance on using technology to teach languages. This has become an important and very accessible source of information for teachers.

# Other websites

Each chapter in this book also has a list of useful websites, including some school and LA websites, on a variety of themes linked to Primary Languages. You will need to check these links to ensure that they are still 'live' and also add to the list as you discover new sources of online support.

# Useful links

- The League for the Exchange of Commonwealth Teachers (www.lect.org.uk)
- Teachers' International Professional Development (www.teachernet.gov.uk/professionaldevelopment/tipd))
- Department for Children, Schools and Families (www.dcsf.gov.uk/languages)
- National Curriculum guidelines (www.nc.uk.net/nc_resources/html/about_NC.shtml)
- Key Stage 2 Framework for Languages (www.standards.dfes.gov.uk/primary/languages)
- Languages Ladder (www.dfes.gov.uk/languages/DSP_languagesladder.cfm)
- Asset Languages (www.assetlanguages.org.uk)
- Twelve questions you may want to ask (www.nacell.org.uk/cdrom/questions.pdf)

**FURTHER READING** FURTHER READING **FURTHER READING** FURTHER READING

Martin, C. with Farren, A. (2006) *Working together. Native speaker assistants in the primary school.* Young Pathfinder 12. London: CILT. Provides practical suggestions for working with a range of native speaker assistants, including trainee teachers from abroad participating in the multi-lateral Primary Languages ITT Initiative.

De Silva, J. and Satchwell, P. (2004) *A flying start. Introducing early language learning.* Young Pathfinder 11. London: CILT.

# Useful websites

www.lfee.net – provides information about the annual immersion courses in France

www.sunderlandschools.org/international/alphaindex.htm – provides suggestions for organising events such as the European Day of Languages

# Appendix 1
# Intercultural Understanding –
# suggestions for classroom activities

## IU 3.1 Increase awareness of linguistic and cultural diversity
- Ask children what they already know about the languages spoken in the UK.
- Visit www.bbc.co.uk/languages/european_languages/countries/index.shtml, the BBC Languages across Europe website, and click on the UK button. Discover how many languages are spoken in the UK and why. If you click on the hyperlinks you can find out more about the languages spoken in the UK and listen to some.
- Explore and discuss what children already know about the languages spoken in different European countries. BBC Languages across Europe lists the countries together with the languages spoken in each.
- Help children discover some greetings in other languages. Visit voyager.jpl.nasa.gov/spacecraft/languages/languages.html, the NASA Voyager website which gives sound files of greetings in 55 languages. Allow the children to say which languages they would like to hear and try to mimic some of the phrases.
- Make a welcome poster.

## IU 3.2 Locate the country/countries where the language to be studied is spoken
- Using a globe or an atlas, ask children to predict where they think the language is spoken. Using maps allow the children to see the UK in relation to the target language country. Can the children name any countries near the UK? What countries do they already know?
- http//mcps.google.co.uk/ gives an easy to read map that can be moved with the mouse. How many countries can children remember?
- Before and after holidays, invite children to bring in photos, postcards or souvenirs from the different countries where the language is spoken. What did they hear/see/eat/smell/touch?

## IU3.3 Identify social conventions at home and in other cultures
- Talk about the conventions of politeness when greeting people such as bowing, shaking hands, kissing on cheeks.

## IU 3.4 Make indirect or direct contact with the country/countries where the language is spoken
- Have contact with a native speaker (including peers in the class or school).
- Watch a DVD or video of native speaker (children) – several published resources have delightful authentic clips of children and adults in school settings.
- See if there is a native speaker within the local community who would be willing to visit your school.
- Link with a partner school in the particular country. Look at the etwinning website: www.etwinning.net.
- Send emails, letters or postcards to the school/class.
- Link national festivals to the school assembly.
- Send an E-Easter card. www.kidlink.org/italiano/progetti/kidart/cards/cards_easter.htm.

## IU 4.1 Learn about festivals and celebrations in different cultures
- Organise a theme day on a particular celebration, e.g. a saints day. Find out about traditional stories,

food, music, costumes, artwork. Prepare for the theme day by getting children to create posters. Make a video diary and compare and contrast your school's theme day with video footage of the real celebration.

- Learn how children of different cultures celebrate special days.
- Invite visitors to school to put on a dance workshop or tell a story.
- Children can consider the festival of Christmas, as well as other festivals celebrated among different cultures in the UK. The BBC has information about the festivals of Christmas, Diwali, Eid, Ramadan, Hanukkah, the Ten Ages of Christmas, Christmas carols. Children could also find out what happens on 6 December (Saint Nicolas) by way of celebration.
- Draw up a calendar of key festivals and learn about how these festivals are celebrated in other countries.
- Find out about how young people spend Christmas www.myeurope.eun.org/ww/fr/pub/myeurope/home/schools/inside/inside/insidetest
- French website www.joyeuse-fete-com/calendrier.html has links to explain festivals of many faiths and key dates.
- For information on the festival of San Fermin in Spain go to – www.spanish-fiestas.com/spanish-festivals/pamplona-bull-running-san-fermin.htm or www.spanish-fiestas.com/video/pamplona-bull-run.htm
- www.sanfermin.com gives you information about the town of Pamplona.
- Children can work together to produce a multilingual happy birthday banner. Each child is given a pennant shaped flag and must decorate it and write happy birthday in a different language. Phrases in a wide range of languages can be found at www.shabbir.com/romance/bday.html

## IU 4.2 Know about some aspects of everyday life and compare them to their own

- Investigate facts such as how old children are when they start school, what a breakfast routine is like in the foreign country, and hold a 'French' breakfast.
- If you have a partner school, email the school with an account of your school's daily routine and compare with their account of start times, school dinner routines, playtimes, days when children go to school and days which they have at home.
- Find out how children get to and from school at the beginning and end of the school day.
- Find out about the holidays and what children typically do as leisure activities.
- In contrast, investigate what work different parents or carers do and the kinds of jobs available in the country or countries where the language is spoken.

## IU 4.3 Compare traditional stories

- Choose a story which is already familiar to the children in English and find the same book in the chosen language. Listen to the story in the language being learned.
- Compare characteristics of simple stories between cultures www.joyeuse-fete-com/calendrier.html. For French traditional tales go to the following websites: www.racontine.com, www.momes.net, fslactivities.sd61.bc.ca/stories.html.
- Tales by the Brothers Grimm in English and German can be found at www.pitt.edu/~dash/grimmtales.html.
- Look at the writing system of the language.

## IU 4.4 Learn about ways of travelling to the country or countries

- In groups, select one of the countries and mark the route from home to the destination.

## IU 5.1 Look at further aspects of their everyday lives from the perspective of someone from another country

- View some video clips preferably with a commentary. On the second viewing, divide the class into two – one half considers what they can see is the 'same' and the other half looks at what is different. Divide the children into pairs with one child from each half. Invite the pairs to present what they have noticed to the group.

- Imagine what a child whose first language is not English feels like when coming to stay with a family or arriving in school in the UK for the first time. Consider how the child might react. In pairs, role play the situation and discuss ways of supporting the new arrival and avoiding misunderstandings and fear.

### IU 5.2 Recognise similarities and differences between people and places

- Liaise with a school in the appropriate country. Find out about places of interest and key buildings and geographical features.
- Write a travel brochure for visitors – get the temperature from a daily newspaper.

### IU 5.3 Compare symbols, objects or products which represent their own culture and those of another country

- Learn about symbols representing children's own country, culture and community.
- Learn about symbols and products from another country and culture.
- Create two shoeboxes: one which the class feels represents their own culture, one which they feel represents the culture of the partner school. Send it to the partner school. Ask them to do the same. Compare what they send you with what you have sent them. The discussion that arises will confront stereotypes.
- Have big sets of objects, symbols, pictures such as fish and chips, *croissants,* the Queen, Big Ben, bagpipes, a rugby ball, football. Ask children, in groups, to sort out the objects and pictures into the country which they represent. Which ones overlap – rugby and football?
- Use a Venn diagram with hoops. Invite children or parents who have been to other countries to talk about their visit and highlight things which are the same and things which are different.

### IU 6.1 Compare attitudes towards aspects of everyday life

Attitudes towards mealtimes and food, lunchtimes in England and other countries, food differences. Saturday morning school. Different timings for school. French cycling – *Tour de France – boules,* cricket does not really exist.

- Find out about attitudes towards similar topics in your partner school.
- Make a list of role models and identify why they have been chosen by the children. Find out about role models from partner schools.

### IU 6.2 Recognise and understand some of the differences between people

- Discuss how language learning can help to improve understanding across cultures.

### IU 6.3 present information about an aspect of culture

- Perform songs, plays and dances.
- Use ICT to present information about another culture having a greater sense of audience.

  La musique                  http://uk.360.yahoo.com

  http://www.blogger.com.start

# Useful websites for Intercultural Understanding

http://maps.google.co.uk/

http://maps.google.co.uk/maps

http://myeurope.eun.org/ww/en/pub/myeurope/home.htm

http://www.joyeuse-fete.com/accueil.html

# Appendix 2
# Developing your own Intercultural Understanding

## TDA bilateral initial teacher training project/Echange franco-britannique

*Observations pendant la formation croisée à Paris*

Compléter le profil de l'école et les notes d'observation ciblées.
Que remarquez-vous sur les thèmes suivants?

la journée

l'emploi du temps

les rôles de l'école/le rôle des adultes dans l'école par exemple :
le directeur/la directrice                       les professeurs

l'organisation pédagogique

le milieu scolaire

le comportement des élèves

la politesse

les habitudes culinaires

Autres

### Observations linguistiques/langage pédagogique pour gérer la classe et le comportement des élèves.

**Que dit le professeur pour...**

faire rentrer les enfants dans la salle de classe

attirer l'attention des élèves

demander de s'installer

faire l'appel

contrôler les déplacements

changer le calendrier: date/jour/temps/anniversaires

présenter les activités

mettre les élèves en groupes

demander de travailler indépendamment

distribuer du matériel

ramassser du matériel

féliciter

réprimander

donner les devoirs

ramasser les devoirs

parler du travail

évaluer le travail dans les cahiers d'exercice

faire sortir à la récréation

à la fin du cours

ranger les affaires

le vocabulaire en général

le vocabulaire spécifique (français, maths, calcul, sciences, etc)

Autres expressions utiles

# Appendix 3
# Guidelines for teaching grammar and KAL

- Teach the new language in a linguistic and cultural *CONTEXT*
- Stress MEANING as well as FORM: Grammar involves using language at sentence and text level
- PLAN what you want children of different abilities to know
- SELECT: which new vocabulary? Which new structures?
- SEQUENCE: what order?
- ONE difficulty at a time
  combine NEW grammatical points with FAMILIAR language
  |  |  |
  |---|---|
  | NEW VOCAB | *KNOWN STRUCTURES* |
  | NEW STRUCTURES | *KNOWN VOCAB* |
- Move beyond CHUNKS
- Help children become AWARE OF PATTERN

SHOW PATTERNS VISUALLY  *COLOUR coding*
*OVERLAYS*
*COLUMNS*
*WORDS INTO CATEGORIES*
*ARROWS TO SHOW LINKS*
*CIRCLES*
*POWER POINT*
*DIFFERENT COLOURED BOXES/MATS/HOOPS for DIFFERENT OBJECTS*

Provide cards, realia, OHT cut-outs/interactive whiteboard items for children to physically handle, sort, move

- Make GRAPHEME PHONEME LINKS and apply them regularly encourage children to become LANGUAGE DETECTIVES
- ASK QUESTIONS:
  What do you notice? What can you hear that's different?
  Can you see/hear a pattern? What do all these words have in common? Why have I been saying X?
- Help children formulate PROVISIONAL RULES: Can someone give me a rule?
- EXPLAIN in simple language using COGNATES and grammatical TERMINOLOGY from En/Literacy/KS2 Framework to summarise
- Do ACTIONS for different word classes
- Do lots of PRACTICE in a fun way through games, songs, problem solving/thinking activities
- Provide opportunities for children to re-use grammatical patterns/rules
- Build up a class record in a systematic way, perhaps using ICT with examples, some of children's own choosing. Use DISPLAY
- Discuss LANGUAGE LEARNING STRATEGIES explicitly with children. How are they going to memorise new words? What helps them remember patterns? Encourage children to check their writing.
- Continually circulate material – Revise – in a fun way –
- *next lesson     next week     next month*
- *next term     next year etc*

# Appendix 4

## European Language Portfolio activity

| |
|---|
| Listening and understanding |
| Speaking |
| Talking to someone |
| Reading and responding |
| Writing |
| Intercultural understanding |
| I have made contact with someone from a different country |
| I can understand my teacher's instructions |
| I can play Simon Says |
| I read an email message |
| I can count from 1–10 |
| I can write a short dialogue |
| I can name some animals |

| |
|---|
| I can ask where someone lives |
| I have learned about some traditional celebrations at home and abroad |
| I can sing a song |
| I can write a postcard |
| I can understand someone asking questions about my name, age and where I live |
| I can say how I am |
| I can name several languages |
| I can read some labels in a matching game |
| I can write an email message |
| I can read a short dialogue |
| I have learned a song from a different country |
| I can match words which I hear with pictures |
| I can say the months |
| I can label objects |
| I can follow someone else's conversation |
| I know how to greet someone politely in at least two languages |
| I can do actions to a story as I hear it |

| |
|---|
| I can read a postcard |
| I can say a rhyme |
| I can write my name, age and where I live |
| I can ask someone's name |
| I can read the names of some objects |
| I can say if I have brothers and sisters |

# Appendix 5
# A new paradigm for languages 7–14

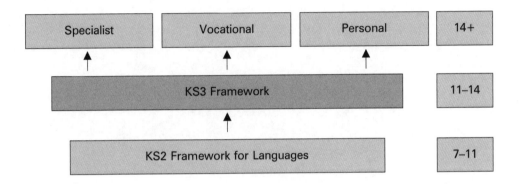

# Appendix 6
# Useful websites and links

## Clipart, visuals and images, teaching resources

www.primaryresources.co.uk/mfl
free resources created by teachers for sharing in French, German, Spanish and Italian

www.primaryresources.co.uk/mfl/douze.htm

www.primaryresources.co.uk/mfl/lesnombres.htm

www.primaryresources.co.uk/mfl/keysamples/unit%2o5%20L%27anniversaire.pdf

www.primaryresources.co.uk/mfl/keysamples/VOL%20101%20Flashcards1.pdf

www.primaryresources.co.uk/mfl/colourgame.htm

www.primaryresources.co.uk/mfl/multisensory.htm

www.primaryresources.co.uk/mfl/keysamples/unit%203%20les%20couleurs.pdf

www.primaryresources.co.uk/mfl/keysamples/unit%203%les%20peintres.pdf

www.primaryresources.co.uk/mfl/slapsnap.htm-minitwisterboard

http://web.uvic.ca/hcmc/clipart
3000 simple non-language specific images for a variety of languages

www.sparklebox.co.uk
Key Stage 1 and Key Stage 2 resources mainly linked to literacy and numeracy but some for
French and a sharing page

## Sites linked to schools

www.downs.kent.sch.uk/default.shtml
French and German resources

www.languagesonline.org.uk
Royal Grammar School High Wycombe
Includes primary French drag and drop activities which children can play and self correct
Also some simple German and Italian (linked to curriculum on-line)

www.Ashcombe.surrey.sch.uk
has downloadable free resources for primary languages

# Art and craft activities for children

http://auxpetitesmains.free.fr/

http://auxpetitesmains.free.fr/Paques.htm

www.cartables.net
http://cartables.net/ecoles/region.php
French site with information on schools

www.cartespourenfants.com
French speaking children's site with colouring, craft activities, interactive games, French and English, self correcting age range 0–10

www.fr.coloriage.com/
practise colours in French

http://atschool.eduweb.co.uk/rgshiwyc/school/curric/French/primary/colours/index.htm

www.chezmerlin.com
French maths games site website

www.teteamodeler.com
craft activities, recipes, colouring, French instructions for festivals during year etc

www.zut.org.uk interactive activities for French from Year 7 (subscription for school use during the day but free from 4 p.m-9 a.m). Separate site and subscription for German. There is now a FREE junior zut site for French which you access from the home page

www.kidzfun.de/
German: some useful recipes

http://sierra.mimic.net/ressources.htm

# Songs, rhymes and stories

www.momes.net
French site with stories

www.racontine.com

http://www.mamalisa.com/world/index.html
songs from around the world especially English and Spanish, audio files, lyrics

www.thierry-klein.nerim.net
French songs with audio files

http://ngfl.northumberland.gov.uk/languages/
interactive stories in French and German such as Red Riding Hood, Goldlilocks and others

www.1001contes.com/contes.php
French site with lots of stories including audio

www.itscotland.org.uk/mfle/sharingpractice/drama.asp
plays in French, German and Spanish

http://new.craftpacks.co.uk
lots of finger and hand puppets and masks for traditional stories

www.mantralingua.com
multilingual dual language books

# Games

www.teachingideas.co.ukforeignlanguages.contents.htm
teaching ideas, activities and games submitted by teachers, adaptable to a number of languages

www.teachingideas.co.uk/foreignlanguages/duckduckgoose.htm

www.teachingideas.co.uk/foreignlanguages/countingaround.htm

www.teachingideas.co.uk/foreignlanguages/teachingnumbers.htm

www.linguacentral.co.uk
links to language games

www.uptoten.com
on-line games in French

www.kidsweb.de
Children's site all in German with puzzle, games, art and crafts

www.spielstrasse.de
in German, puzzles, games, cultural information take a trip to world countries, recipes

www.bbc.co.uk/schools/primary/french
BBC Primary French site free

# Intercultural Understanding

www.dea.org.uk
Education charity which promotes global learning in the school curriculum

www.globalgateway.org.uk
bringing the international dimension to education, gateway to educational partnerships

www.globalgateway.org.uk/default.aspx?page=2842

www.globalgateway.org/projects

www.globalgateway.org/curriculum
lesson plans, ideas for 4-7 and 8-11, festivals and special days section with ideas for assemblies for each week of the school year

## DCSF International Schools Award and overseas partnerships

www.globalgateway.org/isa
Recently relaunched in three tiers, Foundation, Intermediate and Full Award

www.etwinning.net
School partnerships in Europe based on ICT

www.epals.com/
global community of connected classrooms

www.bbc.co.uk/worldclass/find/index.shtml
Guidance on e-twinning

www.bbc.co.uk/worldservice/learningenglish/communicate/worldclass/pdfs/wc_userguide.pdf
Finding a twin

http://www.myeurope.eun.org/ww/fr/pub/myeurope/home/schools/inside/insidetest.htm
links to schools

www.sunderlandschools.org./international/for_schools_partnerfinding.htm
Information on the international dimension, including 15 ways to find a partner school

www.sunderlandschools.org/international/alphaindex.htm
many links to other websites

www.elanguages.org/project_group.php?resourcecategoryid=4
links for projects for pupils age 5+ (includes My day at primary school)

http://www.kidlink.org/kie/nls/contents.html
Getting children round the world together on joint projects

www.ltscotland.org.uk/mfle/sharingpractice/nations/linksabroad/creatinglinksabroad.asp

www.teachernet.gov.uk/wholeschool/healthandsafety/visits
advice on organizing educational visits

## European Day of Languages

www.cilt.org.uk/edl

www.britishcouncil.org/learning-world
termly news magazine with free subscription from the British Council

www.britishcouncil.org/comenius
Opportunities for partnerships, in-service training, becoming and hosting a Comenius assistant (who is generally considering teaching as a possible career)

www.languageassistant.co.uk
information on becoming or hosting a Foreign Language Assistant, including links to Primary FLA starter pack

# DCSF Teachers' International Professional Development

www.teachernet.gov.uk/tipd

# Festivals and linguistic diversity

www.worldeventsguide.com
what's happening around the world countries, cities, themes, today, tomorrow, next week, any time.

www.shabbir.com/romance/bday.html
happy birthday phrases in many languages

http://ngfl.northumberland.gov.uk/crosscurricular/euro/default.htm
All about the euro plus flag games and other activities

http://www.newburypark.redbridge.sch.uk/langofmonth/
Video clips of children from this school teaching their own language

# France

http://www.allo-languages.org.uk/french_sites.htm
Bilingual site for young learners exploring the web (presented by ALL)

www.universdelulue.free.fr/tonanniversaire.html
stories, songs, activities, including fêtes spéciales.

www.joyeuse-fete.com/calendrier.html
details of les fêtes – all in French

www.joyeuse-fete.com/saint-nicolas.html

www.joyeuse-fete.com/joyeux-noel
Christmas activities

www.noel.tourisme-alsace.com
text in French for teachers

www.britishcouncil.org/languageassistant-primary-easter.htm

www.kidlink.org/italiano/progretti/kidart/cards/cards_easter.htm
E-Easter cards

www.fete-enfants.com/
French site with information on special days such as Mother's Day, art and craft activities

www.funsocialstudies.learninghaven.com/edu/mothers-day.htm

www.chiff.com/a/st-josephs-day.htm
Father's day

www.itscotland.org.uk/mfle/sharingpractice/seasons/index.asp

# Sport

http://fr.sports.yahoo.com/football/equipe-de-france/
variety of sports: tennis, basketball, cycling, Olympics, rugby, Formula One, football, includes photos of team players, scores

www.simple.wikipedia.org/wiki/list_of_french_football_teams

www.letour.fr
cycling in France

# Food

www.tourdefromages.co.uk
A–Z of French cheeses and the regions they come from

www.socialstudiesforkids.com/subjects/frenchrevolution.htm
Information in English about cultural, geographical and historical topics

www.socialstudiesforkids.com/articules/holidays/bastilleday.htm
information plus fun things to do and cards to send

www.carnaval.qc.ca
bi-lingual site about the Quebec Ice Festival

www.learnalberta.ca
info on Alberta, Canada

# Spanish

http://www.allo-languages.org.uk/spanish_sites.htm

http://www.fcbarcelona.com/web/index_idiomes.html

www.sanfermin.com

www.spanish-fiestas.com/spanish-festivals/pamplone-bull-running-san-fermin.htm

www.spanish-fiestas.com/video/pamplona-bull-run.htm

www.spanish-fiestas.com/recipes

www.spanish-fiestas.com/flamenco

www.spanish-fiestas.com/art

www.anacleta.homestead.com

# Local weather

http://weather.weatherbug.co.uk
to compare weather where your school is with elsewhere – local weather by postcode

# Germany

www.goethe.de
In German with English text options

www.eduweb.vic.gov.au/languagesonline
Australian website (University of Victoria) with paper based and interactive activities in French, German, Italian and Indonesian. Downloadable songs. Also downloadable templates to create your own multi media language games.

www.japan21.org.uk/teachers/resources/activitiychest.html
Japanese resources from the Japan Society, formerly Japan 21

www.jpf.org.uk/language/library.php
loan by post service from Japan Foundation London Language Centre

www.ipl.org/youth/cquest/northamerica/northamerica.html

www.digitaldialects.com
free activities for learning languages, geography, names of religions, range of languages top KS2 or KS3

# Knowledge about language

www.petlanguages.co.uk/primaryoverview.asp
investigating languages Multilingual approach to languages course in four levels

http://www.language-investigator.co.uk/

www.bbc.co.uk/languages/french/family/
for parents to use with their children learning languages

# Subscription sites

www.enchantedlearning.com
French, German, Spanish, Italian activities

www.enchantedlearning.com/crafts/mardigras/

www.enchantedlearning.com/themes/Frenchshtml

www.linguascope.com

www.taskmagic.co.uk

# Games

www.atantot.com/ks2presente.htm

www.quia.com
Create your own resources and games

www.lcfclubs.com
French and Spanish, includes Babelzone (subscription) with 300 songs and activities

# Purchasable resources

www.singinFrench.com
Song CDs to purchase

www.younglinguists.com
Young Europeans Bookstore part of European Bookshop in Warwick Street London

www.littlelinguist.co.uk
stickers, books, CDs in variety of languages

www.amazon.fr
French books, especially Ecole des loisirs

www.milanpresse.com
story books and magazines and books to prepare children for school

www.posterpals.ca
French and Spanish materials

www.amazon.de
German books

# Language improvement

www.bbc.co.uk/languages/italian/tutors/index.shtml

www.bbc.co.uk/languages/french/tutors/index.shtml

www.bbc.co.uk/languages/german/tutors/index.shtml

www.bbc.co.uk/languagse/spanish/tutors/index.shtml

www.aboutfrench.com

www.byki.com

before you know it teachers' site for learning languages

www.francaisfacile.com

http://lexiquefle.free.fr/learn-french.htm

www.learn.co.uk/defalt.asp?

Guardian on-line service

# Glossary

**ALL: Association for Language Learning** A national, independent subject association representing languages in all sectors. Founded in 1990 from the merger of existing foreign language subject associations. See www.all-languages.org.uk.

**Assessment** The measurement of a child's progress, can be **formative** or **summative**, an integral part of teaching. Assessment opportunities need to be planned into lessons.

**Asset Languages** An awarding body to recognise and accredit achievement in language learning in discrete skill areas for learners of all ages and abilities. Provides external testing for the **Languages Ladder**, the national recognition scheme devised for languages, and one of the outcomes of the **National Languages Strategy**. See www.assetlanguages.org.uk.

**ATs: Attainment targets** The four skills of listening and responding, speaking, reading and responding, and writing as related to language learning.

**CILT: The National Centre for Languages** Formerly the Centre for Information on Language Teaching and Research. See www.cilt.org.uk.

**Cohort** All the children in a year group.

**CLIL: Content and Language Integrated Learning** The use of the new language as a means of instruction in order to teach some content via the medium of the language.

**Continuity** The links from previous learning to new learning, so that previous experience informs the next stages of learning.

**Continuous assessment** The act of measuring children's progress over time rather than as a one-off occurrence.

**CPD: Continuing professional development** Ongoing training during your career to ensure that your skills and knowledge are maintained, refreshed and updated.

**Cross-curricular** The teaching of areas of knowledge and skills through integrating them into a number of other aspects of classroom work.

**Cross-phase** Moving through school from one key stage to another, particularly going from the primary to the secondary sector; arrangements for representatives from two different phases, for example, primary and secondary, to work together 'cross-phase'.

**DELL: Developing Early Language Learning** Generally refers to the projects which succeeded the ELL Initiative between 2001 and 2003.

**DCSF: Department for Children, Schools and Families**.

**DfES: Department for Education and Skills**.

**Differentiation** The process of considering the needs of individual children and ensuring that they are given learning tasks which help them make appropriate progress.

**EAL: English as an Additional Language**.

**eLearning** Electronic teaching and learning resources based on information technology.

**ELL: Early Language Learning** Pre-11 language learning. One way of describing Primary Languages and in particular the DfES/CILT ELL Initiative from 1999–2001.

**ELLAF: Early Language Learning Advisory Forum** (replaced the PLN).

**ELP: European Language Portfolio** A record keeping document for children based on the Common European Framework. A Junior version, My Languages Portfolio, has been published by CILT.

**Entitlement** A nationally recommended, non-statutory element of the curriculum.

**ETML: Early Teaching of a Modern Language** Name given to languages projects in primary schools during the 1980s and 1990s.

**Every Child Matters** (2004) Government programme for a national framework to support the 'joining up' of children's services. It states that every child, whatever their background or circumstances, should have the support they need to be healthy, stay safe, enjoy and achieve, make a positive contribution, and achieve economic well-being.

**Excellence and Enjoyment** see The Primary National Strategy.

**FL: foreign language** Language not experienced outside the classroom.

**Formative assessment** Assessment to help to diagnose the strengths and areas for development of learners so that focused activities can be planned to address their learning needs. The emphasis on positive feedback (two stars) and an area to develop (a wish), so that children know what to do to improve and move forward. Also known as Assessment for Learning (AfL).

**Framework** National government guidelines for a subject.

**HEI: Higher Education Institution** Usually the part of a university which offers initial teacher education as well as professional development for teachers, together with higher degrees.

**Inclusion** The right of every child to be able to access the curriculum in a way appropriate to their needs and interests. Part of the Every Child Matters directive.

**INSET: In-service education and training.**

**Intercultural Understanding** The development of children's and teachers' understanding and appreciation of other cultures together with enhanced awareness of their own culture. One of the three main strands of the Key Stage 2 Framework for Languages.

**ITE: Initial Teacher Education.**

**ITT: Initial Teacher Training.**

**KAL: Knowledge about Language** Knowing and understanding how language and languages work, including vocabulary and grammatical structures and patterns as well as language awareness.

**KS1: Key Stage 1** Reception to Year 2, ages 4–7.

**KS2: Key Stage 2** Year 3–6, ages 7–11.

**KS3: Key Stage 3** Year 7–9, ages 11–14.

**L1** First or native language, mother tongue.

**L2** Second language, generally acquired naturally.

**LA: local authority** Formerly LEA, local education authority.

**Languages Ladder** Part of the National Languages Strategy languages recognition scheme, introduced to extend opportunities for learning languages. The Languages Ladder consists of six stages, with grades within each stage. The first stage, Breakthrough, is particularly appropriate for language learners in primary schools.

**Learning objectives** The three main strands in the Key Stage 2 Framework for Languages: Oracy, Literacy, Intercultural Understanding.

**League table** An instrument for comparing and publishing the results of national tests in the core subjects of English, maths and science.

**Learning style** The most effective method for an individual to access and process learning.

**Literacy** Reading and writing. The second of the three main strands of the Key Stage 2 Framework for Languages.

**LLS: Language Learning Strategies** The processes which successful language learners adopt in order to learn effectively. One of the two cross-cutting strands of the Key Stage 2 Framework for Languages.

**MFL: Modern foreign languages.**

**ML: Modern languages.**

**MLPS: Modern Languages in the Primary School** (Primary languages in Scotland.)

**NACELL: National Advisory Centre on Early Language Learning** A key outcome of the ELL Initiative in 1999, based at CILT as well as via the website, www.nacell.org.uk. NACELL is being brought together under www.primarylanguages.org.uk.

**NAHT: National Association of Head Teachers.**

**NALA: National Association of Language Advisers** Founded in 1969.

**NFER: National Foundation for Educational Research.** www.nfer.org.uk.

**New language** Expression used in the Key Stage 2 Framework for Languages to mean what secondary languages teachers call the target language; the new language being learned.

**Non-statutory subject**. An area of the curriculum which is not mandatory. There is no legal requirement to teach it although it is recommended.

**NQT: Newly Qualified Teacher.**

**OFSTED: Office for Standards in Education.**

**Oracy** Speaking and listening. One of the three main strands in the Key Stage 2 Framework for Languages.

**P6: Primary 6** Sixth year of primary schooling in Scotland, ages 10–11.

**P7: Primary 7** Seventh year of primary schooling in Scotland, ages 11–12 (children remain in primary school in Scotland one year longer than in England).

**Pedagogy** The act and art of teaching and learning.

**PL: Primary Languages.**

**PLN: Pre-11/Primary Languages Network.**

**PMFL: Primary Modern Foreign Languages** A way of describing Primary Languages.

**PPA time: Planning, preparation and assessment time**. Since September 2005 all teachers with timetabled commitments are entitled to 2.5 hours or half a day a week non-contact time.

**Policy** The decisions made by those with strategic oversight of education about what is taught, by whom and when.

**PoS: Programme of study** Curriculum outline.

**Primary National Strategy** On 20 May 2003 *Excellence and Enjoyment*: **A Strategy for Primary Schools** was published, setting out the vision for the future of primary education.

**Prior learning** Work undertaken by children in earlier years or previous schools.

**QCA: Qualifications and Curriculum Authority.**

**QTS: Qualified Teacher Status.**

**S1: Secondary 1** First year of secondary schooling in Scotland, ages 12–13.

**S2: Secondary 2** Second year of secondary schooling in Scotland, ages 13–14.

**Strands** In the context of Primary Languages, the five strands in the Key Stage 2 Framework for Languages are Oracy, Literacy, Intercultural Understanding, Knowledge about Language and Language Learning Strategies.

**Summative assessment** Sums up the total progress that a child has made over a period of time. Often in comparison with others in the cohort.

**Target language** The foreign language being taught. An expression used by secondary languages teachers, in contrast to new language, used in primary documentation.

**TDA: Training and Development Agency for Schools** Formerly TTA, Teacher Training Agency.

**Total physical response** Children engaging in activities, including gesture, to accompany and aid learning.

**Transition** Children moving between classes, year groups or key stages. In particular, going from primary to secondary school.

**VAK** Refers to visual, aural and kinaesthetic learning styles and incorporates total physical response.

# References

Alexander, R. (2000) *Culture and pedagogy. International comparisons in primary education*. Oxford: Blackwell Publishing.

Assessment and Reform Group (2002) Assessment for learning: Ten principles. Research-based principles to guide classroom practice. www.qca.org.uk/libraryAssets/media/4031_afl_principles.pdf.

Association for Language Learning (1992) *Policy statement on an earlier start to Foreign Language Learning.* Rugby: ALL.

Ausubel, D. (1964) Adult versus children in second language learning: psychological considerations. *Modern Language Journal*, 48.

Bell, E. with Cox, K. (1996) Integrating a modern language into the infant school curriculum, in Hurrell, A. and Satchwell, P. (eds) *Reflections on modern languages in primary education: six UK case studies*. London: CILT.

Black, P. and Wiliam, D. (1998) *Inside the Black Box: raising standards through classroom assessment.* London: King's College.

Blondin, C., Candelier, M., Edelenbos, P., Johnstone, R., Kubanek-German, A. and Taeschner, T. (1998) *Foreign languages in primary and pre-school education*. London: CILT.

Bolster, A., Balandier-Brown, C. and Rea-Dickins, P. (2004) Young learners of modern foreign languages and their transition to the secondary phase: a lost opportunity? *Language Learning Journal*, Winter 20 04 30: 35–41.

Brown, K. and Brown, M. (2003) *Reflections on citizenship in a multilingual world*. London: CILT.

Buckby, M. (1976) Is Primary French in the balance? *Audio Visual Language Journal* 14, 1: 15–21.

Burstall, C., Jamieson, M. Cohen, S. and Hargreaves, M. (1974) *Primary French in the balance.* Slough: NFER.

Byram, M. (1989) *Cultural studies in foreign language education*. Clevedon: Multilingual Matters.

Byram, M. (1994) *Teaching and learning language and culture*. Clevedon: Multilingual Matters.

Byram, M. (1997) *Teaching and assessing intercultural communicative competence*. Clevedon: Multilingual Matters.

Byram, M. and Doyé, P. (1999) Intercultural competence and foreign language learning in the primary school, in Driscoll, P. and Frost, D. (eds) *The teaching of modern foreign languages in the primary school.* London: Routledge.

Byram, M. and Zarate, G. (1997) Definitions, objectives and assessment of socio-cultural competence, in Byram, M., Zarate, G. and Neuner, G., *Socio cultural competence in language learning and teaching*. Strasbourg: Council of Europe.

Canale, M. (1993) From communicative competence to language pedagogy, in Richards, J.C. and Schmidt, R.W. (eds) *Language and Communication*. Longman.

Cheater, C. and Farren, A. (2001) *The literacy link*. London: CILT.

CILT (1995) *Modern Languages in primary schools. CILT report*. London: CILT.

CILT (2006) *Positively plurilingual. The contribution of community languages to UK education and society.* London: CILT.

Clarke, S. (2001) *Unlocking formative assessment.* London: Hodder and Stoughton.

Collier, V. P. (1989) How long? A synthesis of research on academic achievement in a second language. *TESOL Quarterly* 23 (3): 509–31.

Council for Subject Associations (CfSA) (2008) *Primary Subjects*, Issue 1.

Council of Europe (2001) *Common European Framework of reference for languages learning, teaching and assessment.* Cambridge: Cambridge University Press.

Curtain, H. and Pesola, C.A. (1994) *Languages and children: making the match.* New York: Longman.

Dearing, R. (1993) *The National Curriculum and its assessment.* London: SCAA.

Dearing, R. and King, L. (2006) Languages Review. *A Consultation Report.* Nottingham: DfES publications.

Dearing, R. and King, L. (2007) *Languages Review.* Nottingham: DfES publications.

DCSF (2007) *Key Stage 2 Framework for Languages. Part 3.* Nottingham: DCSF publications.

DES (1990a) *National curriculum modern foreign languages working group: Initial advice.* London: HMSO.

DES/Welsh Office (1990b) *Modern Foreign Languages for ages 11–16: Proposals of the Secretary of State for Education and Science and the Secretary of State for Wales.* London: HMSO.

DfEE (1995) *Modern Foreign Languages in the National Curriculum.* London: HMSO.

DfEE (1998) *The National Literacy Strategy.* London: DfEE.

DfEE (1999) *The National Numeracy Strategy.* London: DfEE.

DfEE/QCA (1999a) *National Curriculum non-statutory guidelines for MFL.* London: DfEE.

DfEE/QCA (1999b) *The National Curriculum Handbook for primary teachers in England.* London: DfEE.

DfES (2002) *National Languages Strategy, Languages for all: languages for life.* Nottingham: DfES publications.

DfES (2003a) *Excellence and enjoyment: A strategy for primary schools.* Nottingham: DfES publications.

DfES (2003b) *Speaking, Listening and Learning: working with children at Key Stage 1 and Key Stage 2.* Nottingham: DfES Publications.

DfES (2004) *Every Child Matters: change for children.* Nottingham: DfES publications.

DfES (2005) *Key Stage 2 Framework for Languages. Parts 1 and 2.* Nottingham: DfES publications.

Donaldson, M. (1978) *Children's minds.* London: Fontana.

Downes, P. (2002) The untapped potential of language awareness. Presentation at Language World Conference, University of York.

Downes, P. (2007) Language awareness. Presentation at Language World Conference, University of Oxford.

Downes, P. (2008) Multilingual-language awareness. Presentation at Language World Conference, University of Oxford.

Driscoll, P. (1999) Modern foreign languages in the primary school: a fresh start, in Driscoll, P. and Frost, D (eds) (1999) *The teaching of modern foreign languages in the primary school.* London: Routledge.

Driscoll, P., Jones, J. and Macrory, G. (2004) *The provision of foreign language learning for pupils at Key Stage 2. DfES Research Report 572.* Nottingham: DfES publications.

Edelenbos, P. and Johnstone, R. (eds) (1998) *Researching languages at primary schools: some European perspectives.* London: CILT.

Erler, L. (2007) Finding out about learners' approaches to written French through the development of a strategies questionnaire. *Language Learning Journal* 35 (2): 141–152.

European Commission COM (1995) 590 *Teaching and Learning. Towards the Learning Society.* White Paper on Education and Training.

European Commission COM (2003) 449 *Promoting Language Learning and Language Diversification: An Action Plan (2004–2006).*

European Commission COM (2005) 596 *A New Framework Strategy for Multilingualism.*

Eurydice (2005) *Key data on teaching languages at school in Europe.* Eurydice European Unit/European Commission. Available at www.eurydice.org.

Gamble, C. J. and Smalley, A. (1975) Primary French in the balance. Were the scales accurate? *Modern Languages* 94 (7): 94–97.

Gardner, R.C. and Lambert, W. E. (1972) *Attitudes and motivation in second language learning.* Rowley, Mass: Newbury House.

Gregory, A. with Hicks, S. and Comfort, T. (2003) Citizenship and modern foreign languages in the primary school, in Brown, K. and Brown, M. (eds).

Grenfell, M. (2007) Language learner strategy research and modern foreign language teaching and learning. *Language Learning Journal* 35 (1) 9–22.

Grenfell, M. and Erler, L. (2007) Language learner strategies. *Language Learning Journal* 35 (1) 5–7.

Grenfell, M. and Harris, V. (1999) *Modern languages strategies in theory and practice.* London: Routledge.

Harris, V. (2007) Exploring progression: reading and listening strategy instruction with near-beginner learners of French. *Language Learning Journal* 35 (2): 189–204.

Harris, V. and Grenfell, M. (2004) Language learning strategies: a case for crosscurricular collaboration. *Language Awareness* 13 (2) 116–130.

Hawkins, E. (1981) *Modern languages in the curriculum.* Cambridge: Cambridge University Press.

Hawkins, E. (1984) *Language awareness in the curriculum: an introduction.* Cambridge: Cambridge University Press.

Hawkins, E. (1987) *Modern languages in the curriculum.* Cambridge: Cambridge University Press.

Hawkins, E. (ed) (1996) *Thirty years of language teaching.* London: CILT.

Hoy, P. H. (ed) (1977) *The early teaching of modern languages.* London: Nuffield Foundation.

Hunt, M., Barnes, A., Powell, B., Lindsay, G. and Muijs, D. (2005) Primary modern foreign languages: an overview of recent research, key issues and challenges for educational policy and practice. *Research Papers in Education* 20 (4): 371–390.

Hymes, D. (1971) *On communicative competence.* Philadelphia PA: University of Pennsylvania Press.

Johnstone, R. (1994) *Teaching modern languages at primary school.* Edinburgh: Scottish Council for Research in Education.

Johnstone, R. (2003) Evidence-based policy: early modern language learning at primary. *Language Learning Journal*, 28: 14–21.

Jones, B. (1995) *Exploring otherness.* London: CILT.

Jones, J. and Coffey, I. (2006) *Modern foreign languages 5–11. A guide for teachers.* London: David Fulton.

Krashen, S. (1984) *Principles and practice in second language acquisition.* Oxford: Pergamon Press.

Low, L. (1999) Policy issues for primary MFL in Driscoll, P. and Frost, D., (eds). 50–63.

Low, L., Brown, S., Johnstone, R. and Pirrie, A. (1995) *Foreign languages in Scottish primary schools: evaluation of the Scottish pilot projects 1993–1995. Final report to Scottish Office*. University of Stirling: Scottish CILT.

Low, L., Duffield, J., Brown, S. and Johnstone, R. (1995) *Foreign languages in Scottish primary schools*: *Evaluation of the Scottish pilot projects*. Stirling: Scottish CILT.

Macaro, E. (2007) Do near beginner learners of French have any writing strategies? *Language Learning Journal*, 35(1): 23–36.

Martin, C. (2000a) *An analysis of national and international research on the provision of modern languages in primary schools.* Report for Qualifications and Curriculum Authority. London: QCA.

Martin, C. (2000b) Modern foreign languages at primary school: a three-pronged approach? *Language Learning Journal*, 22: 5–10.

Martin, C. (2001) Early MFL learning for the millennium. *Education 3–13*, 29 (2): 43–48.

Martin, C. (2002) *Rhythm and rhyme. Developing language in French and German.* London: CILT.

Martin, C. (2006) *Interim evaluation of the Languages Bridge project* 2005–2006. University of Reading.

Martin, C. (2007) *Final evaluation of the Languages Bridge project* 2006–2007. University of Reading.

Martin, C. with Cheater, C. (1998) *Let's join in. Rhymes, poems and songs.* Young Pathfinder 6. London: CILT.

Martin, C. with Farren, A. (2006) Working together. Native speaker assistants in the primary school. London: CILT.

Martin, C. and Mitchell, R. (1993) Foreign language assistants in the primary school. *Language Learning Journal*, 8: 32–34.

Mitchell, R. (2003) Rethinking the concept of progression in the National Curriculum for Modern Foreign Languages: a research perspective. *Language Learning Journal*, 27: 15–23.

Mitchell, R. and Dickson, P. (1997) *Progression in foreign language learning*. University of Southampton. Centre for Language in Education occasional paper 45.

Mitchell, R. and Martin, C. (1997) Rote learning, creativity and 'understanding' in classroom foreign language teaching. *Language Teaching Research*, 1 (1): 1–27.

Mitchell, R. and Myles, F. (1998) Second language learning theories. London: Arnold.

Mitchell, R., Hooper, J. and Brumfit C. (1994) *Final report: 'Knowledge about language', language learning and the national curriculum*. University of Southampton Centre for Language in Education. Occasional papers 19.

Mitchell, R., Martin, C. and Grenfell, M. (1992) *Evaluation of the Basingstoke primary schools language awareness project 1990/1991*. University of Southampton: Centre for Language in Education, Occasional Paper 7.

Molzan, J. and Lloyd, S. (2001) *Le manuel phonique*. Essex: Jolly Learning Ltd.

Moys, A. (Ed) *Where are we going with languages?* Nuffield Languages Inquiry. London: Nuffield Foundation.

Muijs, D., Barnes, A., Hunt, M., Powell, R., Arweck, E., Lindsay, G. (University of Warwick) and Martin, C. (University of Reading) (2005) *Evaluation of the Key Stage 2 Language Learning Pathfinders. Research Report 692.* Nottingham: DfES publications.

Muir, J. (1999) Classroom connections, in Driscoll, P. and Frost, D. (eds) *The teaching of modern foreign languages in the primary school.* London: Routledge.

Naiman, N., Fröhlich, M., Stern, H. H. and Todesco, A. (1978) *The good language learner*. Clevedon: Multilingual Matters.

National Association of Head Teachers (1992) *Modern Languages in the Primary School: Conference Resolution*. West Sussex: NAHT.

Nisbet, J. and Shucksmith, J. (1986) *Learning strategies*. Routledge.

Nuffield Foundation (2000) *Languages: the next generation. The final report and recommendations of the Nuffield Foundation Languages Inquiry*. London: Nuffield Foundation.

Oller, J. and Nagato, N. (1974) The long-term of FLES: an experiment. *Modern Language Journal*, 58: 15–19.

O'Malley, J. and Chamot, A. U. (1990) *Learning strategies in second language acquisition*. Cambridge: Cambridge University Press.

Pollard, A. (2005) *Reflective teaching*. Continuum: London.

Poole, B. (1994) Modern languages in the primary school curriculum. A critical evaluation. Unpublished MA thesis. London: Institute of Education.

Poole, B. (1995) The unseens traps of random experiences. *Times Educational Supplement Extra*, vi.

Powell, R., Wray, D., Rixon, S., Medwell, J., Barnes, A. and Hunt, M. (2001) *Analysis and evaluation of the current situation relating to the teaching of modern foreign languages at Key Stage 2 in England*. London: QCA.

Primary Languages Network working party (1996) *The Introduction of Foreign Languages into the Primary School Curriculum*, Draft 4, London: CILT.

Qualifications and Curriculum Authority (2000) *Scheme of Work for French, Spanish and German*. London: QCA.

Qualifications and Curriculum Authority (2001) *QCA project to study the feasibility of introducing the teaching of a modern foreign language into the statutory curriculum at Key Stage 2*. Available on-line at www.qca.org.uk/libraryASsets/media.3807_mfl_feas_ks2.pdf.

Qualifications and Curriculum Authority (2007) *Scheme of work for French, German and Spanish*. London: QCA.

Radnai, Z. (1996) English in primary schools in Hungary, in P. Edelenbos and R. Johnstone (eds) *Researching languages at primary school: Some European perspectives*. London: CILT.

Rixon, S. (1992) English and other languages for younger children: practice and theory in a rapidly changing world. *Language Teaching*, 25 (2): 73–93.

Rubin, J. (1990) How learner strategies can inform language teaching. In V. Bickley (ed) *Language use, language teaching and the curriculum*. Hong Kong: Institute of Language in Education.

SCAA (School Curriculum and Assessment Authority) (1997) *Modern Foreign Languages in the primary curriculum: an international conference*. London: SCAA.

Schumann, J. H. (1975) Affective factors and the problem of age in second language acquisition. *Language Learning*, 25: 209–255.

Schumann, J. (1978) The acculturation of L2 acquisition, in R. Gingras (ed) *Second language acquisition and foreign language teaching*. Arlington W Virginia: Center for Applied Linguistics, 27–30.

Sharpe, K. (1991) Primary French: More phoenix than dodo now. *Education 3–13,* 19 (1); 49–53.

Sharpe, K. (2001) *Modern Foreign Languages in the primary school*. London: Kogan Page.

Sharpe, K. (2003) *Evaluation of Good Practice project/DELL (2001–2003)*. London: CILT.

Singleton, D. (1989) *Language acquisition and the age factor*. Clevedon: Multilingual Matters.

Skarbek, C. (1997) *First steps to reading and writing*. London: CILT.

Skarbek, C. (2005) Presentation at ITT conference.

Skarbek, C. (2008) Handout for trainees.

Stern, H. H. (1975) What can we learn from the good language learner? *Canadian Modern Language Review*, 31: 304–318.

TDA/CILT (2008) Teacher Trainee Support Material for QCA A Scheme of Work for Key Stage 2 French. London: TDA/CILT.

Tahta, S., Wood, M., and Loewenthal, K. (1981) Age changes in the ability to replicate foreign pronunciation and intonation. *Language and Speech,* 24 (4): 363–372.

Tierney, D. and Hope, M. (1998) *Making the link*. London: CILT.

Trafford. J. (ed) (1992) *Primary Foreign Languages: a fresh impetus*. Proceedings of ALL/NAHT Conference, Coventry. Rugby: ALL.

Walters, S. (2007) Researching Bangladeshi pupils' strategies for learning to read in (UK) primary school settings. *Language Learning Journal*, 35 (1): 51–65.

Wiegand, P. (1992) *Places in the primary school*. London: Falmer Press.